Praise for *Your Team Can Soar!*

"For over 20 years, Wes Friesen has bee
ership in articles, in classrooms and in speeches. With *Your Team Can Soar!* Wes brings together the best of his ideas on leadership, management and teamwork. An excellent resource for new and experienced managers."

Mark Fallon
CEO, Berkshire Company

"This book is:
  Powerful!
  Profound!
  Practical!

Each chapter is a gem full of so much theoretical and useful wisdom it will blow you away. Wes Friesen has somehow distilled massive amounts of research down to the nuts and bolts that make leadership work. Not only is this a fun book to read, but it can also be a textbook and a reference volume which you will return to over and over again. If you lead people or work with people in any way, you need this book."

Dr. Steve Stephens
Psychologist, professor, conference speaker, author of 28 books

"What I love about *Your Team Can Soar!* is that every single chapter is to-the-point, insightful and cuts right to the heart of what makes for great managers in the most practically important areas of team leadership. Wes Friesen writes as someone who is an expert in leadership theory, but more importantly understands how to make it work with real people in real life."

Mike Fleischmann
Vice President, Missions Door - Denver, Colorado

"Wes has created a great mosaic of leadership and management principles in a single tome. He makes the case that leadership and management are sourced in a solid personal foundation. Having been fortunate to have Wes on my management team and Brad Fishel as our internal consultant, I have experienced the result and reward as these principles are lived and strengthened daily through the lives of work teams."

Bruce Carpenter
Vice-President Distribution, Retired, Portland General Electric

"Wes Friesen combines the wisdom of successful leaders and teachers, inspirational quotes, and stories from his own career to deliver leadership guidance sorely needed in many businesses today. He backs up his advice with decades of research by distinguished experts. Friesen not only tells managers what to improve and why they should, he gives specific direction about how to do it."

Mike Porter

President, Print/Mail Consultants and author of *Take This Job* and *STUFF It*

Steve,
wish you the Best!
Soar!
Wes F...

Your Team CAN SOAR!

*Powerful Lessons to Help You Lead
and Develop High Performing Teams*

Wes Friesen

Your Team Can Soar!
Powerful Lessons to Help You Lead and Develop High Performing Teams
by Wes Friesen

Printed in the United States of America.

ISBN 9781498460866

www.xulonpress.com

Dedication and Acknowledgements

This book is dedicated to you, the reader. I aspire to be a servant leader and developer of people. One of my passions related to this aspiration is to share useful information with motivated adult learners like you. I truly hope that by learning and applying some of the concepts from the book, you will be more successful - and add greater value to your team and key stakeholders.

I have been fortunate to work with many great executive leaders that have modeled the way for me and other aspiring leaders. A partial list included in this category are Peggy Fowler, Jim Piro, Mike Fleischmann, Loren Fischer, Arleen Barnett, Joe McArthur, Steve Hawke, Chris Ryder, Bill Nicholson, Bruce Carpenter and Kristin Stathis.

I have also enjoyed working with and learning from many peers, and those that have been a part of my leadership teams. An incomplete list includes Jerry Rhoades, Bruce Trout, George Kuiawa, Behzad Hosseini, Elyssia Lawrence, Rick Van Beek, Eric Houger, Matt McHill, Josh Bigelow, Heidi Fouts, Allison Rowden, Jessica Eberhardt, Dave Worth, Michaela Lynn, Garret Saiki, Kathy Philips-Israel, William Tierney, Beth Smith, Shawneen Betha, John

Kauffman, Rob Wiggins, Larry Frick, Phil Steckmann, Greg Peterson and Ed Gann.

A special thanks to organizational learning and development experts DeAngela Wells and Brad Fishel for freely sharing of their knowledge and expertise.

I have enjoyed speaking at conferences and interacting with industry experts like Mark Fallon, Mike Porter, Jim Mullan, Barbara Fahy, John Joachim, Mike Lathrop, Paul Dreifuss, Ron Goglia, Nick Stafferi, and Jim Burns.

I am also grateful for those who have provided me opportunities to teach, speak and write over the years. Included in this group recently are Amanda Armendariz, Bob Neubauer, Francis Ruggiero, Lance Humphries, Bruce Gay, Peggy Smith, Richard Boudrero, Jean Gauthier, Jill Leimbach, Brian Shappell, and Jack Lyda.

I want to say thank you to author Glenn Hoerr for his encouragement and insights. Thank you to Psychologist, author and friend Dr. Steve Stephens for sharing his wisdom, and thanks to my editor Laura Davis for cleaning up my manuscript.

None of my accomplishments would be possible without the support and encouragement of my best friend and wife, Debi. I am also blessed and inspired by my daughters Amy and Alyssa, son-in-law Keith and granddaughter Taylor.

Finally, I want to express appreciation to the ultimate Servant Leader, who provides me inspiration, purpose and the help to get worthwhile things done.

I hope you enjoy the book and mine out some nuggets of value!

Contents

Introduction

"... to learn and not to do is really not to learn.
To know and not to do is really not to know."
—Stephen R. Covey

I have had the privilege of helping to lead, manage and develop a number of high performing teams in my career. I have also been blessed to have the opportunity to share information with motivated adult learners in a variety of channels; in the university classroom, at conferences and through the pages of several trade journals. The purpose of this book is to put into one place important information that can help you be even more successful in leading, managing and developing high performance teams.

Using this as a reference book you can periodically study a top-ic(s) and pull out some key concepts to apply. These 42 lessons are intended to be "stand-alone" and can be used for your personal development as well as the development of your teams. Many lessons contain information you already know, but as Greek philosopher Plato said, "The greater part of instruction is being reminded of things you already know." Everyone in some form of leadership or management role can benefit from the contents of this book, as can those that aspire to leadership roles. There is also useful information for those not interested in leadership roles, but who are interested in developing their personal skills and abilities.

The book is segregated into three sections based on the three parts of a Management model developed by Organization Development expert Brad Fishel. Below is a simplified copy of Brad's Management model:

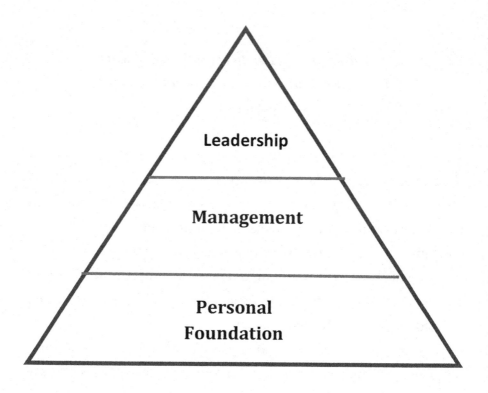

Part One is focused on *Leadership*. This section includes lessons related to leadership philosophies, leadership practices and leadership qualities and traits.

Part Two looks at *Management*. This section covers a wide range of important management practices that are essential to managing and developing high performance teams.

Part Three provides insights on *Personal Foundations*. This eclectic range of lessons addresses a variety of important skills, abilities and behaviors that are important for our personal success—and our success as leaders.

Throughout the book you will see many references and quotes from a wide range of people. This is intentional. I take to heart the advice found in Proverbs, including " ... Wise men and women listen to each other's counsel," "Many advisors make victory sure," and "Become wise by walking with the wise" (excerpts from Proverbs 11:14, 13:10 and 13:20). There are smarter, wiser and more successful men and women from which we can learn. At the end of the book I have included a suggested reading list for those who want to dig deeper into what others have to say about leadership and management.

I wish you the best of success as you continue on your journey to continually become an even more effective leader, manager and developer of high performance teams!

PART ONE:
LEADERSHIP LESSONS

"No individual achievement can equal the pleasure of leading a group of people to achieve a worthy goal. When you cross the finish line together, there's a deep satisfaction that it was your leadership that made the difference. There's simply nothing that can compare with that."

—Bill George, former CEO of Medtronic

1

Are You a Serving Leader or a Self-Serving Leader?

"Everyone can be great, because everyone can serve."
—*Dr. Martin Luther King, Jr.*

O rganizations and teams are crying out for effective leaders. The most effective and positive leaders are those that understand and practice the philosophy of "servant leadership". Servant leaders feel their role is to serve others—employees, customers and other key stakeholders. If you think about the most respected and effective leaders you know, chances are they saw themselves as "serving leaders", not "self-serving leaders". The most notable leaders throughout history, such as Gandhi, Martin Luther King, Nelson Mandela and Mother Teresa, embraced the philosophy stated by Jesus, "Anybody wanting to be the leader must first be the servant. If you want to lead you must serve."

One of my favorite definitions of leadership is "leadership is the skill of influencing people to work enthusiastically towards goals that are identified as being for the common good". Do you want to be an influential leader? I suggest learning and applying the following

"SERVE" model, based on Ken Blanchard's *The Secret: What Great Leaders Know and Do*:

- **S**ee the Future
- **E**ngage and Develop Others
- **R**einvent Continuously
- **V**alue Results **and** Relationships
- **E**mbody the Values

See the future involves developing a compelling vision that stirs passion within you—and the people on your team. Invite participation from your team members about your team's purpose, values and goals. Consider how you can add value for your key stakeholders, such as customers, employees and shareholders/owners. Give serious thought to where you and the team would like to be several years in the future—then paint a picture of a better future that people can rally around.

Engage and develop others involves having the right people in the right roles, fully engaged to achieve the future. Identify a person's strengths (refer to the "Strengths Interview" found in the lesson #10 *Best Practices of Great Managers*) and find a role that leverages those strengths. I agree with Peter Drucker who said, "The leader's objective is to leverage the strengths of people and make their weaknesses become irrelevant." We have many tools available to help develop people, including classes, cross training, special assignments, mentoring, and the list goes on.

Reinvent continuously is based on the concepts of continuous learning and continuous improvement. Learning and improvement start with us first. We need to read, attend conferences, be involved with professional organizations, and model the behavior for team members. We need to regularly evaluate our systems and processes and keep asking, "Can we do it better, faster and for less? Can we improve the quality of our products and services?"

Value results and relationships. Our job as leaders is to get results that add value to the organization and its stakeholders. But how we get results is very important. Servant leaders realize that people are our most valuable resource, and developing positive relationships is absolutely essential. Servant leaders know that "people will not give you their hand until they see your heart."

I try to live out my "3 Rs" approach with people in my life: **Recognize** people for who they are and for what they do, **Reward** in tangible and intangible ways whenever you can, and show **Respect** and practice the golden rule.

Embody the values that you and your organization deem important. A great example is how my employer (Portland General) survived and even thrived, despite being owned by Enron. Our common values were the glue that kept us focused and together: Be Accountable, Dignify People, Make the Right Thing Happen, Positive Attitude, Team Behavior and Earn Trust. Values can drive the corporate culture and provide a strong foundation for developing your vision.

Being a servant leader is rewarding for the people you serve, and for you. Let me close with a quote from Dr. Albert Schweitzer: "I don't know what your destiny will be, but one thing I do know. The only ones among you who will be really happy are those who will have sought and found how to serve."

(Note: Bruce Carpenter has developed a one-page SERVE diagram based on Blanchard's model. You can download it for free from my website *wesfriesen.com*. Look under Handouts/SERVE Leadership diagram)

2

Love Works

"Leading with love is the best way to run an organization.
Any organization."
—Joel Manby, CEO of Herschend Family Entertainment

Want to be a more effective leader? Want to help your team be even more successful? Learning how to consistently lead with love is the key you are looking for. It's one thing to want to lead with love, and another to know how to do it and then live it out. Awhile back I read an outstanding book that can help us. Let me share some of the key ideas.

Joel Manby, CEO and author of *Love Works*

"Undercover Boss" is one of my favorite shows and usually ends with me choked up with emotion. Some of the CEOs featured are already caring and inspiring leaders, others less so, but all end up learning valuable lessons when they work with front line staff and supervisors and realize that people are truly the most valuable resource of any organization.

I remember watching the episode featuring Joel Manby, CEO of Herschend Family Entertainment, which owns or operates about 20 family themed attractions across the country such as Dollywood, Silver Dollar City, and Stone Mountain in Georgia. After seeing Joel on the show I told my wife that this guy really understands what servant leadership is all about, and knows how to add value to all of an organization's key stakeholders (employees, customers, owners and community). I had heard that Joel had just written a book on leadership called *Love Works*, so I got my copy and read it with great interest.

"Leading with Love"

Joel and other successful likeminded leaders understand and promote the concept of servant leadership and "leading with love". Talking about "love" in business makes some people squirm. Part of the problem is that our English language has only one word for love. Our friends the ancient Greeks had four, one of which is "agape" love, which is the one that is most relevant for business settings.

Agape love is not about feelings and is not emotion based. Agape love is unconditional and is behavior based—it's about choosing to care and following up with actions. When we look at love in action, *love works* at work. And it can be a powerful tool to help us strengthen our teams and improve the value we add to our stakeholders.

Key principles that explain this kind of love come from one of the oldest and most respected authorities on human behavior: the Bible. Joel elaborates on seven key principles of practical love that the Apostle Paul outlined in chapter 13 of his first letter to the Corinthians. This is a passage that is often used at weddings, but it can also be used as a leadership philosophy.

Seven Key Principles of Leading with Love

Following are the seven key principles behind leading with love:

1. **Be patient—demonstrate self-control in difficult situations.** Key points include don't be patient with poor performance, but be patient with how you respond with poor performance. Praise patiently in public—including being specific, exact and legitimate. Admonish in private with specifics, then reaffirm the person's value and help them "get back on the horse" and move on. Praise more than you admonish. Multiple studies found the ratio should be at least 5 to 1.

2. **Be kind—show encouragement and enthusiasm.** Kindness is the root of encouragement, encouragement leads to enthusiasm, and everyone benefits from enthusiasm. Remember that kindness, encouragement and enthusiasm start with us in leadership roles. When a leader is kind, it will influence front-line employees who will in turn be more likely to treat customers well.

   Every time we contact someone we can make their day better or worse—so make it better. I like the Sam Horn quote: "Anyone who consistently makes you feel bad is not helping you be better." Finally, break through the e-mail clutter and use hand written notes of thanks. Over the years I have received handwritten notes of appreciation from a CEO and also a President of my company. Both notes are framed and will be mementos that I enjoy well into my retirement years.

3. **Be trusting—place confidence in those around you.** Leading with love isn't possible if you don't trust people. And when you trust people, leading will be more effective than ever. Listening carefully is a sign of trust, while interrupting

people is a sign of distrust. Another way to show trust is to avoid micro-managing and let others make decisions they are responsible for. Then we need to avoid overriding a decision that has already been made unless it is absolutely necessary.

4. **Be unselfish—think of yourself less.** Being unselfish doesn't mean thinking *less* of yourself—it means thinking *of* yourself less. Unselfish leaders aim to make as few decisions as possible. They also deploy a Socratic rather than autocratic leading style. Socratic leading involves asking questions, facilitating rich team discussions, and then making the best possible decision based on that rich discussion. Margaret Thatcher has a great quote that supports the Socratic and participative approach: "Being in power is like being a lady. If you have to remind people that you are, you aren't."

5. **Be truthful—define reality corporately and individually.** Highly respected CEO Max DePree said, "The first responsibility of a leader is to define reality." Practical guidelines include: Don't shoot the messenger or confuse disagreement with negative conflict. Don't assume people see the truth—speak up. As a leader, it's usually best to speak last. Be open to hearing the truth. And find an accountability partner or partners that will always tell you the truth about you. Finally remember the adage to "speak the truth in love."

6. **Be forgiving—release the grip of the grudge.** What was done to you doesn't matter in the end. All that matters is how you respond. If someone has wronged your team or organization, consider giving them another chance if it is a one-time offense; they are aware of their shortcomings; they want to improve; and if you have doubts about letting them go.

Forgive someone who has wronged you. I agree with Jeff Henderson who says, "The longer you hold a grudge, the longer the grudge has a hold on you."

7. **Be dedicated—stick to your values in all circumstances.** Choosing to lead with love may be the single most difficult decision a leader can make, but a wise leader dedicates herself to it because it is also the best way to lead an organization. If you lead anything or anyone, you are in a position of power. As leaders we need to use the power given us to get things done such as setting stretch targets, holding others accountable, asking for resources, making tough decisions, rallying people to common goals and getting results. Great leaders do all these things and at the same time lead with love. Martin Luther King Jr. understood this well when he said, "Power without love is reckless and abusive, and love without power is sentimental and anemic." Dr. King understood that love and power must be harnessed together to get the most important things done.

My final encouragement is to follow Gandhi's charge to, "Be the change you want to see in the world." Good luck to you as you follow the path of leading with love and setting a positive example for others!

P.S. For a further discussion of servant leadership, including an overview of the ultimate servant leader, refer to Appendix A, *The Ultimate Servant Leader.*

3

What Kind of Leader are You?

"A good team always outperforms a group of strong but independent individuals. In other words, the whole is greater than the sum of the parts."
— Dr. Gayle Beebe, President, Westmont University
and author of *The Shaping of an Effective Leader*

How do we transform diverse individuals into powerful, high performing teams? One useful tool is to learn and put into practice the Leadership (aka Managerial) Grid model.

What is the Leadership (Managerial) Grid Model?

The **Leadership Grid** model is a behavioral leadership model developed by Robert Blake and Jane Mouton years ago, and validated by researchers and leaders today. This model identifies five different leadership styles based on the *concern for people (relationships)* and the *concern for production (results)*. The optimal leadership style in this model is based on Theory Y, which I write about in lesson #4, *"Are You a Theory X or Theory Y Leader?"*

The Leadership Grid is a practical and useful framework that helps you think about your leadership style. By plotting 'concern for production' against 'concern for people', the grid highlights how placing too much emphasis in one area at the expense of the other leads to low overall productivity. The model proposes that when both people and production concerns are high, employee engagement and productivity increases accordingly. This is often true, and it follows the ideas of Theory Y and other participative management theories.

The Leadership Grid is based on two behavioral dimensions:

- **Concern for People (Relationships)** – This is the degree to which a leader considers the needs of team members, their interests, and areas of personal development when deciding how best to accomplish a task.

- **Concern for Production (Results)** – This is the degree to which a leader emphasizes concrete objectives, organizational efficiency and high productivity when deciding how best to accomplish a task. Using the axis to plot leadership 'concerns for production' versus 'concerns for people', Blake and Mouton defined the following five leadership styles:

The Leadership Styles of the Model

The model is represented as a grid with *concern for production* as the x-axis and *concern for people* as the y-axis; each axis ranges from 1 (Low) to 9 (High). The resulting leadership styles are as follows:

Country Club Leadership: High People/Low Production (1,9)

This style of leader is most concerned about the needs and feelings of members of his/her team. These leaders operate under the assumption that as long as team members are happy and secure then they will work hard. What tends to result is a work environment that is very relaxed and fun but where production suffers due to lack of direction and control.

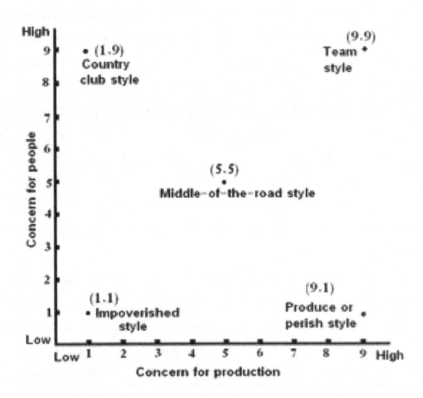

Produce or Perish Leadership: High Production/Low People (9,1)

Also known as Authoritarian or Compliance leaders, people in this category believe that employees are simply a means to an end. Employee needs are always secondary to the need for efficient and productive workplaces. This type of leader is very autocratic, has strict work rules, policies, and procedures, and views punishment as the most effective means to motivate employees. This dictatorial style lines up with McGregor's Theory X.

Impoverished Leadership: Low Production/Low People (1,1)

This leader is very ineffective. He/she has neither a high regard for creating systems for getting the job done, nor for creating a work environment that is satisfying and motivating. The result is a place of disorganization, dissatisfaction and disharmony.

Managers use this style to preserve job security, protecting themselves by avoiding getting into trouble. The main concern for the manager is not to be held responsible for any mistakes, resulting in less innovative decisions.

Middle-of-the-Road Leadership: Medium Production/Medium People (5,5)

This style seems to be a balance of the two competing concerns. It may at first appear to be an ideal compromise. Therein lies the problem, though. When you compromise, you necessarily give away a bit of each concern so that neither production nor people needs are fully met. Leaders who use this style settle for average performance and often believe that this is the most anyone can expect.

Team Leadership: High Production/High People (9,9)

Also now known as "Transformational Leader". According to the model, this is the pinnacle of managerial style and lines up with the Theory Y approach. These leaders stress production needs and the needs of the people equally highly. The premise here is that employees are involved in understanding organizational purpose and determining production needs. When employees are committed to, and have a stake in the organization's success, their needs and production needs coincide. This creates a team environment based on trust and respect, which leads to high satisfaction and motivation and, as a result, high production.

The "Transformational Leader" according to leadership researcher Bernard Bass:

- Is a model of integrity and fairness
- Sets clear goals; Has high expectations
- Encourages; Provides support and recognition
- Stirs people's positive emotions
- Gets people to look beyond their self-interest
- Inspires people to reach for the improbable

Applying the Leadership Grid

Being aware of the various approaches is the first step in understanding and improving how well you perform as a manager. It is important to understand how you currently operate, so that you can then identify ways of becoming competent in both realms.

Step One: Identify your leadership style

- Think of some recent situations where you were the leader.
- For each of these situations, place yourself in the grid according to where you believe you fit. You can also solicit input from people who have worked with you.

Step Two: Identify areas of improvement and develop your leadership skills

- Look at your current leadership method and critically analyze its effectiveness.

- Look at ways you can improve. Are you settling for 'middle of the road' because it is easier than reaching for more?
- Identify ways to get the skills you need to reach the Team (Transformational) Leadership position. These may include involving others in problem solving or improving how you communicate with them, if you feel you are too task-oriented. Or it may mean becoming clearer about scheduling or monitoring project progress if you tend to focus too much on people.
- Continually monitor your performance and watch for situations when you slip back into bad old habits.

Step Three: Put the Grid in Context

It is important to recognize that although the Team Leadership style is generally the most effective leadership approach, there are times that call for more attention in one area than another. If your team is in the midst of a merger or some other significant change, it is often acceptable to place a higher emphasis on people than on production. Likewise, when faced with an economic hardship or physical risk, people concerns may be placed on the back burner, for the short-term at least, to achieve high productivity and efficiency.

I like this quote from Tony Dungy: "The secret to success is good leadership, and good leadership is about making the lives of your team members better." Good luck to you as you make the lives of your team members better by showing a high concern for them as people AND the results they achieve!

4

Are You a Theory X or a Theory Y Leader?

"In the past a leader was a boss. Today's leaders must be partners with their people ... they can no longer lead based solely on position power"
—Ken Blanchard

Want to be a more effective leader? Understanding and properly applying the Theory X & Y leadership model will help. Let's take a look at where Theory X & Y came from and how we can apply it to be better leaders.

Roots and Explanation of Theory X & Y

The theory X &Y leadership model was developed 50 years ago, and has stood the test of time and been validated by modern research. The model was proposed by social psychologist Douglas McGregor in his classic book *The Human Side of Enterprise*. McGregor's model suggests that there are two fundamental approaches to managing people. Many managers tend towards Theory X, and generally get poor results, especially over the longer term. Enlightened managers mostly use Theory Y, which produces better performance and results, and allows people to grow and develop. Let's look at these two competing leadership philosophies:

Theory X (authoritative and traditional style). Theory X managers assume that people are lazy, don't want to work, and it is the job of the manager to force or coerce them to work. People are viewed as a "cost" that must be monitored and controlled. It is based on three basic assumptions:

1) The average person inherently dislikes work and will avoid it if at all possible.
2) Most people have to be coerced, controlled, directed and threatened to get them to work towards organizational goals.
3) The average person prefers to be directed, avoids responsibility, isn't ambitious and simply seeks security.

In practice, Theory X managers tend to be autocratic and controlling, and feel it is up to them to ride people and make them do their work (i.e. managers are "policemen"). These managers tend to micromanage, be extremely task oriented and not put much emphasis on building positive relationships. Little emphasis is shown towards developing a positive work environment, and recognition and appreciation would be rare. People working for these managers tend to be motivated by fear and feel unappreciated. President Dwight D. Eisenhower spoke against this style by stating, "You do not lead by hitting people over the head – that's assault, not leadership."

Theory Y (dignified and enlightened style). Theory Y managers assume people will perform well if treated positively, and that higher order needs dominate most individuals. People are viewed as "assets" that should be valued and developed. It is based on six basic assumptions:

1) The physical and mental effort of work is as natural as play, so the average person does not inherently dislike work.

2) People will exercise self-direction and self-control in order to achieve objectives.

3) Rewards of satisfaction and self-actualization come from the effort to achieve objectives.

4) The average person learns not only to accept but to seek responsibility.

5) Most people have a capacity for imagination, ingenuity and creativity.

6) The intellectual potential of most people is only partially realized.

In practice, Theory Y managers tend to be participative when making decisions, and value both Results *and* Relationships. These managers tend to delegate and empower their people because they trust them and feel they will do good work (i.e. managers are "coaches"). Priorities will be given to developing positive work environments, and expressing regular recognition and appreciation. These managers will also feel that people are important and worth developing. People working for these managers tend to feel appreciated and dignified, and will generally have good morale and feel motivated.

Applying Theory Y

Modern research and your own life experiences validate that generally speaking the Theory Y leadership style will lead to better results, both for your people and you as a Manager. It is important to determine which style of leadership you want to follow—then do it! It can be valuable to get regular feedback through direct questions, surveys and third parties to assess how effective your leadership style is. The bottom line is that most people will respond positively to a Theory Y leadership approach, and it's up to us to provide it!

Let's get specific – how do we practice Theory Y management? Here are a few pointers:

- **Vision and Expectations:** Paint a positive vision of a better future, and be clear about expectations. Express your confidence in your team to be great. I like this quote from John Steinbeck: "It is the nature of man to rise to greatness if greatness is expected of him."

- **Leadership approach:** Be a servant leader, not a "serve me" leader. Minimize differences between the management-staff relationship.

- **Planning & Decision Making:** Be participative, not autocratic. Seek and listen to input from your team members.

- **Communication:** Err on the side of over communication versus under communication. Be honest, realistic and positive—and be a good listener too.

- **Control:** It is important to have policies, procedures and work standards in place so people know how to do their work. Avoid being over-controlling and micro-managing the work. Showing trust in your people will lead to higher morale and motivation. Also, encourage your people to share their ideas and use their ingenuity and creativity to do the work smarter and better serve your team's stakeholders.

- **Recognition:** Work on providing regular informal and formal recognition and appreciation. One recent study found that the ratio of positive (appreciative) statements to constructive statements should be at least 5:1 to maximize relationships and motivation.

Let me close with a quote from Sam Walton: "Outstanding leaders go out of their way to boost the self-esteem of their personnel. If people believe in themselves, it's amazing what they can accomplish." I wish you well as you apply the Theory Y approach and help your people and teams achieve their potential!

5

Best Practices of Effective Leaders

"Everything rises and falls on leadership."
—John C. Maxwell, Leadership author and speaker

Organizations and teams are crying out for effective leaders. General William Creech said it well: "There are no weak platoons, only weak leaders." How can we improve our leadership effectiveness? One tool we have is to learn and apply what research tells us. The two most extensive research projects related to leadership effectiveness ended up with the same conclusions. There are Five Absolutes (best practices) for getting high performance and great results.

I want to share these Five Absolutes with you, and pass along some specific ideas that we have used to put these Absolutes into practice.

Absolute 1
Get everyone on the same page:
Focus on the purpose of the organization.

Create and maintain a clear focus on desired results for yourself, your people and your operations as a whole, while creating a means to measure progress and performance. One key I have found can be summarized in the following saying of mine: "You can choose to be mediocre, or you can choose to strive for excellence ... the choice is yours." The default choice if we are not intentional is to settle for mediocrity. I suggest that to be a High Performance leader we must intentionally choose to pursue excellence ... and to make that choice a reality we must develop and communicate the Vision to everybody within our organizational team. John C. Maxwell was right when he said, "Great vision precedes great achievement."

My operations at Portland General have been blessed by receiving positive national recognition. The teams involved have worked hard and smart to make positive changes, and create additional value for our company and its internal and external customers. One thing we did was to articulate an intentional desire to excel. For example, here is a sample Mission and Values statement from one of my operations (Printing & Mail Services):

Mission:

Our mission is to be a "world class" provider of Printing and Mailing products and services. We desire to be recognized as a premier service provider that is comparable to any operation of similar size anywhere in the country.

Our purpose is to provide timely, high quality products and services at a cost equal to or lower than any other potential provider. We desire to achieve a consistently high level of customer satisfaction, and to maintain a working environment that dignifies and motivates our staff.

Values:

- We place a high importance on customer satisfaction. We want to meet and even exceed customer expectations. Quality of our products and services is a priority. We are results oriented and will do what it takes to get the job done.

- We believe our most important asset is our people, so we strive to treat each person respectfully and to train, develop and promote a positive work environment. We believe in being professional, empowering our employees and also having fun.

- We believe in the Total Quality Management concept of "continuous improvement", and are constantly striving to improve all aspects of our operations. We also believe in "continuous learning", and are constantly striving to learn more about best practices, technology, and ways to better meet our customer's needs.

Absolute 2
Prepare for battle:
Equip your operation with tools, talent and technology.

This absolute includes progressively staffing your operation with high-quality people, developing effective planning practices, providing on-going training and education for your people, and ensuring people have the tools they need to get the job done.

Some people have found the following 3 "Ps" keys to operational excellence as a helpful guide. To excel in an operation, we must continuously learn and continuously improve in these key areas:

1. **Physical Assets & Technology** (try to be "leading edge" but not "bleeding edge")

2. People (people are the most valuable resource of any organization)

3. Practices (learn and apply best practices)

An on-going challenge for all operational leaders is justifying the resources we need to excel and add value to our organizations. Let me share some tips that have proven useful. I go into more detail on these tips in lesson #25 *Justifying Resources: An On-going But Winnable Battle.*

Wes' 10 Tips for Justifying Resource

1. Identify important goals and business needs of your organization, then figure out how to help meet them.
2. Find ways to save your organization money.
3. Know your costs and how they compare to the external market.
4. Work with vendors for creative ideas to improve your operations and justify resources.
5. Partner with other departments in your organization.
6. Develop positive relationships with internal "service providers" that influence decisions.
7. Take the budgeting process and other "bean counting" tasks seriously.
8. Understand your organization's capital budgeting and approval system and process.
9. Track your volumes and document increases.
10. Excel in operations and enhance your team's reputation.

Absolute 3
Stoke the fire for performance:
Create a climate for results.

To be effective leaders, we must create an operational climate that provides ongoing performance measurement and feedback, motivates people, and removes barriers to performance in an ongoing and systematic fashion.

One essential ingredient to create the climate we desire is to remove the fear of making occasional, inconsequential mistakes. The reality is that we all make mistakes, and mistakes can actually be helpful if we learn from them and avoid similar mistakes in the future.

The great philosopher Edward Phelps said, "The man who makes no mistakes does normally not make anything." Being a sports fan, I like these quotes from Babe Ruth: "Don't let the fear of striking out get in your way," and Wayne Gretzky: "You miss every shot you do not take."

As leaders, we want to promote calculated risk taking. One of my sayings is, "The wise take calculated risks ... fools take careless risks ... the cowardly take no risks at all." Let's not be careless or cowardly, but master the art of taking calculated risks in striving for better results.

In terms of motivating employees, here are ten ways to help from the Ken Blanchard consulting group:

1) Provide personal thanks.
2) Make time for employees.
3) Provide specific feedback.
4) Create an open (and fun) work environment.
5) Provide information.
6) Involve employees in decisions.
7) Reward high performers (and deal with poor performers).

8) Develop a sense of ownership.

9) Give chances to grow and learn.

10) Celebrate successes.

Absolute 4

Build bridges on the road to results:
Nurture relationships with people.

This Absolute challenges us to identify, foster, nurture and sustain relationships, practice effective communication, and foster cooperation through the practice of trustworthy leadership with the people you need to get results.

To build relationships we must focus on helping others. Jesus was quoted as saying, "It is better to give than to receive." Giving our employees and other people in our lives our "best" will result in stronger relationships:

- Believe in them
- Encourage them
- Support them
- Trust them

Another tool that works is to consistently use the 3 "Rs" when dealing with people:

- **Recognize** (Show appreciation for skills and good performance.)
- **Reward** (Include both monetary and non-monetary rewards.)
- **Respect** (Golden Rule: Treat people positively, as you would like to be treated.)

Absolute 5
Keep the piano in tune:
Practice continuous renewal.

As leaders, we continuously need to improve and renew our-selves, our processes, and our people, and maintain balance in all facets of our lives for long-term success.

I have been inspired by the following quotes:

- *"None will improve your lot, if you yourselves do not"*– Marcus Aurelius
- *"It's what you learn after you know it all that counts"*– John Wooden
- *"There is always room for improvement no matter how long you've been in the business"*–Oscar De La Hoya

The following twin philosophies can be applied to the operations we lead and also to our personal development:

Continuous Improvement: We need to continually strive to get better at what we do. It includes the realization that none of us or the operations we lead are perfect, so there is always room to improve.

Continuous Learning: There is always something new to learn, so keep on learning until the day you cease to exist (i.e., be a "life-long learner"). A great example for me was my Aunt Tina, who was taking correspondence courses until she was 91 — and the only reason she quit was that her eyesight went bad!

John Wooden said, "Perfection is impossibility, but striving for perfection is not." I wish you the best as you continue on your journey to become an even more effective and high performance leader!

6

Vision - The Key to Leadership Success

"There is no more powerful engine driving an organization toward excellence and long-range success than an attractive, worthwhile, achievable vision for the future, widely shared."
—Bert Nanus, author of *Visionary Leadership*

One of the first and foremost responsibilities of successful leaders and managers is developing a vision of a better future for their team. Theodore Hesburgh, President of Notre Dame University, cuts to the chase by saying, "The very essence of leadership is that you have to have a **vision**. It's got to be a vision you articulate clearly and forcefully on every occasion."

Leadership success always starts with a vision. John F. Kennedy famously dreamed of putting a man on the moon. Eleanor Roosevelt envisioned a world of equal opportunity for women and minorities. Henry Ford dreamed of a car families could afford. Steve Job envisioned an easy-to-use computer that would unleash creativity. The vision we have for our teams will not be as world-changing as the examples cited, but can make a world of difference for the teams we are leading.

Extensive research on the Best Practices of High Performing leaders by the University of Michigan found that the best leaders "... get everyone on the same page, and focus on the purpose of the organization." The Gallup organization's research on the practices of the country's greatest managers found that one crucial best practice was to "set expectations, and define the right outcomes." Let's dig into defining what a vision is, discovering the characteristics of a good vision, and some ideas on forming a vision.

What is a Vision?

What is a vision, and what characterizes a good vision? One definition of a vision comes from Bert Nanus, a well-known expert on the subject. Nanus defines a vision as a **realistic, credible, attractive future for an organization**. Let's dissect this definition:

- **Realistic:** A vision must be based in reality to be meaningful for an organization/team. We need to consider the parameters we live within—such as constraints of budget resources, IT support and potential of team members. At the same time, a vision is also *idealistic* in that it paints the picture of a better future and shows what we can be if we all work together for a common aspiration.

- **Credible:** A vision must be believable to be relevant. To whom must a vision be credible? Most importantly, to the employees or members of the organization. If the members of the organization do not find the vision credible, it will not be meaningful or serve a useful purpose. One of the purposes of a vision is to inspire those in the organization to achieve a level of excellence, and to provide purpose and direction for the work of those employees. A vision which is not credible will accomplish neither of these ends.

- **Attractive:** If a vision is going to inspire and motivate those in the organization, it must be attractive. People must want to be part of this future that is envisioned for the organization.

- **Future:** A vision is not in the present, it is in the future. In this respect, the image of the leader gazing off into the distance to formulate a vision may not be a bad one. A vision is not where you are now; it's where you want to be in the future.

Potential Benefits of a Good Vision

Nanus goes on to say that the right vision for an organization — one that is a *realistic, credible, attractive future for the organization* — can accomplish a number of things:

- **It attracts commitment and energizes people**. One of the primary reasons for having a vision for an organization is its *motivational effect*. When people can see that the organization is committed to a vision that points to a better future, it generates enthusiasm and increases the commitment of people to work toward achieving that vision.

- **It creates meaning in workers' lives**. A vision allows people to feel like they are part of a greater whole, and hence provides meaning for their work. The right vision will mean something to everyone in the organization, if they can see how what they do contributes to that vision. Consider the difference between the mail services technician who can only say, "I am a machine operator," to the one who can also say, "I'm part of a team committed to becoming a world class provider of mailing services that is comparable to any operation of similar size anywhere in the country." The work is the same, but the context and meaning of the work is different.

- **It establishes a standard of excellence**. A vision serves a very important function in establishing a standard of excellence. In fact, a good vision is all about excellence. Tom Peters, the author of *In Search of Excellence*, talks about going into an organization where a number of problems existed. When he attempted to get the organization's leadership to address the problems, he got the defensive response, "But we're no worse than anyone else!" Peters cites this sarcastically as a great vision for an organization: "Acme Widgets: We're No Worse Than Anyone Else!"

  A vision so characterized by lack of a striving for excellence would not motivate or excite anyone about that organization. The standard of excellence can serve as a continuing goal and stimulate quality improvement programs, as well as providing a measure of the worth of the organization.

- **It bridges the present and the future**. The right vision takes the organization out of the present, and focuses it on the future. It's easy to get caught up in the crises of the day, and to lose sight of where you were heading. A good vision can orient you on the future, and provide positive direction.

How Do We Develop a Vision?

So how can managers define the right outcomes, set a vision and get everybody on the team on the same page? The 360-degree approach is one wise strategy. Find out where your boss and the *senior management* want the organization to go, and then determine how your team can help them get there. Coordinate with your *peers* and find ways to partner. Solicit participation from your *team members*, as their participation leads to their buy-in and better quality decisions.

Great managers are aware of the concept of "stakeholder symmetry". Stakeholder symmetry recognizes that an organization has multiple stakeholders (e.g. investors, customers, employees, and community). The organization–and your team–should try to add value to each stakeholder, and maintain a reasonable balance between their competing interests.

When developing the Vision, don't forget to answer the "Why" question. The Vision will address "Where" the organization is heading, but we also need to explain the benefits of *why* we are pursuing that future state. I agree with Friedrich Nietzsche, who said, "Given a big enough *why,* people can bear almost any how."

The final outcome for your team should include a Vision or Mission Statement that helps inspire your team to strive for excellence. Following is a sample Vision Statement of the Credit & Collections team at my company:

Vision:

Our vision is to be a "world class" provider of Credit related services. We desire to be recognized as an industry leader in that is comparable to any operation of similar size anywhere in the country.

Our purpose is to provide timely, high quality Credit services which minimize write-offs, and at a cost competitive with any other potential provider. We desire to achieve a consistently high level of customer satisfaction, and to maintain a working environment that dignifies and motivates our staff.

Developing a Vision Statement does not end our leadership responsibility, as Warren Bennis emphasizes by saying, "Leadership is the capacity to *translate vision into reality.* "Here are a few tips to help with the translation of the vision into reality:

Supplement the Vision Statement with annual and quarterly goals, and several performance metrics covering all important areas of performance (e.g. cost, timeliness, quality, customer satisfaction, efficiency, and safety). Review progress on a monthly basis, discuss results with your team, and celebrate improvements and the reaching of goals. The outcome will be a highly motivated team working together for common purposes.

Remember this quote of mine: "You can choose to be mediocre, or you can choose to strive for excellence ... the choice is yours." Good luck as you and your team intentionally strive for excellence!

7

Planning Your Way to a Better Future

"If you don't know where you are going,
you'll end up someplace else."
—Yogi Berra, Yankee Hall-of-Famer and noted philosopher

As I write this lesson I am in the middle of teaching a university course on Strategic Planning. There is no way to cover all the key principles of planning in one short lesson, but allow me to share a few key highlights that may be helpful.

What is the Purpose of Management?

Before digging into some planning principles, let's discuss some foundational management concepts. What is the purpose of management (i.e., why have managers)? Here is a short and simple answer:

*The primary purpose of management is to **effectively** and **efficiently** use organization resources to strive for organizational goals.*

Notice the reminder that the resources we manage (e.g. labor, money, physical assets) are not ours, but the organization's, and that we should be using (managing) them in pursuit of organization goals.

Also, it is helpful to remember the distinction between effectiveness and efficiency. Effectiveness is the degree to which an objective is accomplished ("doing the right things"). Efficiency is maximizing the amount of output for a given quantity of input ("doing things right"). The first priority is to be effective (get the work done), then strive for efficiency without unduly impacting effectiveness.

What is the Purpose of Planning?

Planning is a tool to help management achieve its primary ultimate purpose of achieving organizational goals. Planning is the "means" to set and reach organizational goals ("ends"). Planning is the determination of what is to be done—and of how, when, where and by whom it is to be done. A plan is a predetermined course of action involving the future and involving the action.

Why plan?

The basic purpose is to identify what we want to happen, and then to improve the probability that what we want to happen will happen (i.e. identify our desired future and increase the probability of it occurring).

Planning is essential to being successful. Benjamin Franklin was right when he said, "If you fail to plan, you are planning to fail!"

Here are ten additional benefits that a thoughtful planning process can provide to an organization:

1) Compels management to plan and think ahead; opportunity to look at the future

2) Bases action on thorough investigation, study and research (i.e. improved decision making)

3) Increases management and staff motivation (by establishing standards of performance)

4) Provides basis for resource allocation; makes more efficient use of resources (labor, money and physical assets)

5) Vehicle for senior management to communicate organizational values, goals, strategies and priorities to the entire organization

6) Enhances goal congruence (i.e. goals of individual managers harmonize with goals of organization as a whole)

7) Results in coordinated response to change; increases anticipation and awareness of future threats and opportunities

8) Reveals organization strengths and weaknesses

9) Provides standards for control

10) Allows for subsequent performance reporting and evaluation; provides basis for Performance Indicators

How Do We Plan?

Here are some basic planning principles:

1) Lowest possible relevant units should be involved in the planning process. Goal is participation, which results in "buy-in" and a higher quality plan.

2) Planning should precede action

3) Planning horizon should not exceed the available known resources

4) Plans must be coordinated among related functions

5) Plans must be flexible and recognized as subject to change

6) Plans should be focused on probable future events

To organize your thinking and the planning process, you may find my 3-step Planning Model to be helpful. I have used this simple model in planning for myself, for teams at work, and for non-profit organizations I have been a leader in.

Wes' Planning Model

Step One: Assess the current situation. Ask and answer the question, "Where are we now?" This represents the *Starting Place*. (Note: I recommend completion of SWOT analysis prior to the completion of Step One—see below).

Step Two: Determine your Goals/Objectives to be achieved by the end of the planning period. Ask and answer the question, "Where do we want to go?" This represents our *Destination*.

Step Three: Develop the Strategies that will move you from your current situation (Starting Place) to where you want to go (Destination). These strategies (aka Action Plan) serve as your *Road map*.

SWOT Analysis

Another helpful planning tool is SWOT analysis. Completing the SWOT analysis early in the planning process will help facilitate development of more realistic Goals and Strategies and a higher quality Plan.

SWOT analysis ideally includes input from all the people impacted by the Plan, and involves carefully assessing an organization's:

Strengths. The intent here is to carefully and realistically identify the key strengths of the organization, including relevant strengths about People, Processes and Technology. Strengths are internal based and will help in deciding what opportunities may be realistic to pursue.

Weaknesses. The aim here is to identify the relevant weaknesses of the organization that may impair successful goal achievement or result in Threats to be mitigated. A good starting place is to evaluate where you stand in the areas of people, processes and technology.

Opportunities. Both opportunities and threats should factor in the results of *external analysis*. External analysis considerations can include economic, social, governmental, technological, competitive, and other factors that, combined with the strengths of the organization, could result in opportunities to pursue. For example, if your team has the latest technology and extra capacity—and the external vendors in your area are relatively expensive—you may want to consider pursuing in-sourcing work and add to your organization's bottom line.

Threats. The *external analysis* and analysis of weaknesses can identify threats that need to be addressed. Dealing well with threats will help ensure that your goals and associated strategies are successful.

My final word of advice is to realize that much of the value of planning is in the process, not only in the final plan. President Dwight Eisenhower once stated that, "Plans are nothing; planning is everything." Good luck as you plan your way to a better future for you and your team!

8

Qualities of Effective Leaders

"If you can become the leader you ought to be on the inside,
you will be able to become the person you want on the outside.
People will want to follow you. And when that happens,
you'll be able to tackle anything in this world."
—John C. Maxwell, Leadership author and speaker

B eing an effective leader is critical to the success of your team. In other lessons I discuss the philosophies and the best practices of effective leaders. Let's examine the qualities (or traits) of effective leaders. What are the qualities that effective leaders possess?

In a nutshell, effective leaders are men and women of *character* (who we are) and *competence* (what we can do). Obviously it's hard to narrow down the qualities to one encompassing list, but I have pulled together a list of twenty qualities that can serve as a good starting place.

The list draws from multiple credible sources: Kouzes and Posner's extensive leadership research documented in their book *The Leadership Challenge*; the groundbreaking research by Jim Collins on long-term successful organizations summarized in the book *Good to Great*; the work of the late Warren Bennis, widely considered as one of the leading experts on leadership ever produced, and other experts including Brian Tracy. Here is the list of twenty qualities that effective leaders often exhibit.

Twenty Qualities (Traits) of Effective Leaders

The following list is not in any particular order. There is some overlap between the qualities, and certainly a synergistic effect if a leader possesses all of these traits.

1) **Visionary (Direction)** Effective leaders have a sense of purpose and direction for where they want to lead the organization (team). They have an inspiring vision for a better future for the team. And they can answer the "Big Why" (Why should we change; move from "here" to "there").

2) **Trustworthy** This quality scored the highest in a Gallup survey of what followers wanted from their leaders. Trust is built through relationships and is the foundation for a leader working effectively with her team.

3) **Positive Expectations** The best leaders are optimists who spread their optimism to their teams. Napoleon asserted, "Leaders are dealers in hope." People will tend to rise up to the positive expectations that leaders set for them, especially if there are good relationships in place.

4) **Results Oriented** The most effective leaders focus on achieving worthwhile results. Ken Blanchard was right when he said, "People who produce good results feel good about themselves." One of my cardinal principles is, "Success breeds success." When positive results are achieved and celebrated,

positive momentum is created and teams are inspired to experience more success.

5) **Integrity and Honesty** Kouzes and Posner have been surveying people about what they desire in leaders for two decades. Consistently ranking at the top is "honesty" (closely akin to Integrity). Integrity includes walking the talk and always seeking to do right. Proverbs 10:9 (NIV) advises: "He who walks with integrity walks sincerely, but he who perverts his ways will become known."

6) **Authentic** People are crying out for leaders that are genuine and "real". In recent times we have seen scandals in the business world, in politics, even the non-profit world. Being honest and trustworthy, admitting our mistakes, and asking for forgiveness when appropriate helps us build the sense of authenticity that people crave.

One of the best examples of a leader being authentic happened a couple of years ago at our company's all management meeting. The company was launching an initiative to make safety our company's top priority. Our CEO Jim Piro was explaining the safety initiative, but then went off script. Choked with emotion and eyes filled with tears, he said the bottom line was that he wanted all our employees to go home safe every night, and never wanted to make a call to a home that the employee was severely injured, or not coming home at all. I feel the authentic emotion even writing this, and I guarantee the safety message has stuck with all of us who were at that meeting.

7) **Inspiring** Successful leaders inspire by painting a picture of an appealing better future. And they show how the work done in

the present will lead to the attractive desired future. Sebastian Coe wisely points out that, "Inspirational leaders need to have a winning mentality in order to inspire respect. It is hard to trust in the leadership of someone who is half-hearted about their purpose, or only sporadic in focus or enthusiasm."

8) **Compassion and Empathy** A Gallup survey showed that followers have a strong need for their leaders to be compassionate. People want a supervisor who genuinely cares about them individually. Life is tough, and being treated with compassion and empathy is much appreciated.

9) **Stability** A Gallup survey also found that one of the key qualities people want from their leaders is stability. People appreciate leaders that are emotionally stable and not given to mood swings and excessive displays of negative emotions.

10) **Hope** Hope is another quality that a Gallup survey found people desired in their leaders. People want hope that the future will be better than the present, and what we are doing now will contribute to creating that better future.

11) **Conscientious** I talk about the Big 5 Personality Traits in lesson #32 *Understanding Ourselves and Others.* The one personality trait that most marks successful leaders is a strong sense of being conscientious. A conscientious person is reliable, responsible, organized, dependable and persistent.

12) **Confidence and Decisiveness** The most effective leaders have confidence in their abilities and the abilities of their teams. Effective leaders are also decisive. Successful leaders are humble, delegate often, and rely on the strengths of others. At the same time, when decisions need to be made effective

leaders are decisive and not afraid to make decisions (i.e. the buck stops with them).

13) **Enthusiasm and Passion** Enthusiasm is an endearing quality of effective leaders. Walter Chrysler emphasized the importance of enthusiasm when he said, "The real secret of success is enthusiasm." Ralph Waldo Emerson adds, "Nothing great was ever achieved without enthusiasm." Passion provides the spark and energy to strive for great achievements. John Schnatter, the founder of Papa John's Pizza, encourages us to "Concentrate on what you do well, and do it better than anybody else."

There is a concept called "the shadow of the leader". People will often follow the example a leader sets—so when we exhibit enthusiasm and passion, the people on our teams will tend to follow suit.

14) **Courage** People want leaders to be men and women of courage, not driven by fears. This sometimes means that leaders make unpopular decisions, or decide based on values and convictions not popular at the moment. James Allen admonished, "You will never do anything worthwhile in this world without courage." Winston Churchill adds, "Courage is rightly considered the foremost of the virtues, for upon it, all others depend."

15) **Strategic Thinker/Planner** The best leaders think strategically and can see and explain the big picture. They also understand the concept of stakeholder symmetry and intentionally strive to add value and balance the interests of our key stakeholders–including customers, investors, employees and the community.

16) **Openness/Tolerant of Ambiguity** Openness refers to our ability to be original, creative, curious, daring and take risks. Being tolerant of ambiguity is important because the real world is full of ambiguities, and leaders need to provide leadership even when things are not totally clear and obvious. In a nutshell, effective leaders have the ability to be flexible within the boundaries of their own values and vision for the team.

17) **Communicator** When leaders don't communicate the gap gets filled by the rumor mill, which is primarily negative. Effective leaders communicate well so people know the direction and how things are going. Gilbert Amelio wisely speaks about the importance of communication skills: "Developing excellent communication skills is absolutely essential to effective leadership. The leader must be able to share knowledge and ideas to transmit a sense of urgency and enthusiasm to others. If a leader can't get a message across clearly to motivate others to act on it, then having a message doesn't even matter."

18) **Humor** A sense of humor goes a long way in leadership. Appropriate humor can help create a positive work environment, and enhance the feeling of camaraderie. President Dwight D. Eisenhower emphasized the importance of humor by saying, "A sense of humor is part of the art of leadership, of getting along with people, of getting things done." Business leader Warren Buffet illustrated his own sense of humor when he quipped, "I buy expensive suits. They just look cheap on me."

Robert Half International did a survey and found that 84 percent of executives feel that people with a good sense of humor do a better job. Respondents to a Bell Leadership

Institute survey found that a sense of humor was one of the top two desirable traits in leadership.

19) **Personal Humility** Jim Collins and his team researched long-term high performing organizations and what made them so successful. One common characteristic of these high performing organizations was they were led by "Level 5" leaders. A level 5 leader is marked by two defining characteristics: *personal humility* and at the same time an *intense professional will*.

A level 5 leader is personally humble and not self-absorbed and arrogant. Being humble is attractive to followers, and opens the leader up to listen and respond to other's advice.

20) **Intense Professional Will** This is the second key characteristic of a level 5 leader. In addition to being personally humble, the top leaders possess an intense professional will. They are strongly committed and motivated to lead the organization to achieve worthwhile goals and achieve success. Some classic examples of extreme level 5 leaders include people like Abraham Lincoln, Gandhi and Mother Teresa. My most recent two bosses, Kristin Stathis and Bruce Carpenter, are great examples of leaders with a strong drive and professional will, balanced with personal humility.

Making it Personal

How do you stack up compared to this list? Some of these qualities come more naturally to us, but we can all intentionally strive to improve in the areas we currently fall short. As we improve we will increase our leadership effectiveness, and the people we serve will appreciate the improvements!

9

Leadership Wisdom from King Solomon

"Without good direction, people lose their way; the more
wise counsel you follow, the better your chances."
— King Solomon (Proverbs 11:14 MSG)

K ing Solomon is revered by Christians and Jews as the wisest and most successful earthly leader in scripture. In the Islamic Qur'an he is honored as a prophet. Many have studied his life and writings in order to acquire the secrets of his wisdom. The story of Solomon is recorded in I Kings 1–11, I Chronicles 29 and II Chronicles 1–9. Solomon's writings are contained in Proverbs, Ecclesiastes, and the Song of Songs (aka Song of Solomon).

Solomon was the leader of Israel and led the once embattled and weak nation into a nation of immense wealth and power. He was a masterful financier, military mastermind, master architect and urban planner, and philosophical leader. The Age of Solomon was truly a golden age—four glorious decades where Israel was never so great before or after his reign. We can all learn and apply Solomon's leadership principles and become even more effective leaders. I have summarized 16 leadership lessons from Solomon, so let's dig in and mine out some of his wisdom!

16 Leadership Lessons from King Solomon

1) Seek wisdom and knowledge over fame and fortune.

The first leadership lesson we can learn from King Solomon is that effective leaders seek wisdom and knowledge over fame and fortune (refer to I Kings chapter 3). Soon after Solomon was appointed king of Israel, God appeared to him in a dream and promised to give the young leader whatever he asked for. Solomon asked for wisdom to effectively lead the people of Israel. God blessed the young king for asking for wisdom, and not fortune and fame, and gave him all three.

Many seek leadership roles to make more money and perhaps to make a name for themselves. The effective leader knows that any lasting personal success comes by the way of applied knowledge and wisdom that benefits the organization and its key stakeholders.

"With my (wisdom's) help leaders rule, and lawmakers legislate fairly; with my help, governors govern, along with all in legitimate authority. I love those who love me; those who look for me find me."   —Proverbs 8:15–18 (MSG)

"Get wisdom—it's worth more than money; choose insight over income every time."   —Proverbs 16:16 (MSG)

2) Lead with an inspiring vision for the future and be a good communicator.

Effective leaders inspire and lead through communicating a compelling vision of a better future. George Washington Carver emphasized that, "Where there is no vision, there is no hope." The best leaders develop a purpose and vision that people are inspired to work together to achieve. Charles Noble hit on another benefit of a vision when he said, "You must have a long-range vision to keep you from being frustrated from short-range failures."

"Without a vision, people flounder."   —Proverbs 29:18

"When good people run things everyone is glad, but when the ruler is bad, everyone groans."   —Proverbs 29:2 (MSG)

3) Love your followers and treat them fairly and with compassion.

In the context of leadership, love can be defined as a heartfelt concern for the well-being of others. Enlightened leaders understand that being loving and compassionate towards people builds relationships, and good relationships lead to good results in the workplace.

Pat Williams explains: "A leader loves his followers by caring about their personal, emotional, spiritual, and financial needs; their career advancement; their character growth; their health; and their families. A genuine leader does not view his followers or subordinates as cogs in an organizational machine but as real people with feelings, personal goals, and family relationships." [1]

"Love and truth form a good leader; sound leadership is founded on loving integrity."   —Proverbs 20:28 (MSG)

"Leadership gains authority and respect when the voiceless poor are treated fairly."   —Proverbs 29:14 (MSG)

4) **To be a good leader, become a great motivator and encourager.**

Dr. Bob Nelson, renowned expert on employee motivation, writes: "You get the best effort from others not by lighting a fire beneath them, but by building a fire within them." The best leaders learn and apply ways to help motivate and encourage their followers. One of the keys to help people feel appreciated and motivated is to provide sincere, regular recognition. Margaret Cousins counseled, "Appreciation can make a day— even change a life. Your willingness to put it into words is all that is necessary."

"A good leader motivates, doesn't mislead, doesn't exploit."
                              — Proverbs 16:10 (MSG)

"Do not withhold good from those who deserve it, when it is in your power to act."   — Proverbs 3:27 (NIV)

5) **Recruit and listen to wise advisors.**

Effective leaders recruit wise advisors to counsel them in all matters of the organization. President Woodrow Wilson advised, "We should not only use all the brains we have, but all the brains we can borrow."   Good leaders are not afraid to hire people who know more than them. They are active listeners and humble to follow the advice of their subordinates.

"Arrogant know-it-alls stir up discord, but wise men and women listen to each other's counsel."　　　— Proverbs 13:10 (MSG)

"Refuse good advice and watch your plans fail; take good counsel and watch them succeed."　—Proverbs 15:22 (MSG)

"Take good counsel and accept correction–that's the way to live wisely and well."　　　　　— Proverbs 19:20 (MSG)

6) **Assemble a great team and remove those that don't measure up.**
Industrialist Andrew Carnegie counseled, "No man will make a great leader who wants to do it all himself or get all the credit for doing it." Effective leaders assemble great teams, and remove those members that don't measure up.

"After careful scrutiny, a wise leader makes a clean sweep of rebels and dolts."　　　　　　— Proverbs 20:26 (MSG)

"Like the horizons for breadth and the ocean for depth, the understanding of a good leader is broad and deep. Remove impurities from the silver and the silversmith can craft a fine chalice; remove the wicked from leadership and authority will be credible and God-honoring."　　— Proverbs 25:3-5 (MSG)

7) Focus on quality and excellence.

Vince Lombardi admonished, "The quality of a person's life is in direct proportion to their commitment to excellence, regardless of their chosen field of endeavor." Steve Jobs emphasized, "Be a yardstick of quality. Some people aren't used to an environment where excellence is expected."

"Leaders who know their business and care keep a sharp eye out for the shoddy and cheap."   — Proverbs 20:8 (MSG)

"Remove impurities from the silver and the silversmith can craft a fine chalice."   — Proverbs 25:4 (MSG)

8) Avoid and squelch gossip.

Wise leaders do not participate in gossip and bad mouthing others and do not tolerate those behaviors on their teams. A good example for us was conservative Republican President Ronald Reagan, who was one of the most effective and respected leaders of our generation.

President Reagan was respected even by those on the other end of the political spectrum, like his friend, liberal Democrat House Speaker Tip O'Neil. One of the keys to Reagan's leadership success was that he avoided gossip and belittling others. Reagan's son Ron Reagan once said in an interview, "I never saw him belittle anyone. I have never heard him gossip about anyone or tell stories. He's a nice man to the core and a terribly dignified man ... When you're faced with an ethical decision, perhaps a decision of right or wrong, you could do worse than ask what he might do." [2]

"Trouble makers start fights; gossips break up friendships."

— Proverbs 16:28 (MSG)

"When a leader listens to malicious gossip, all the workers get infected with evil." — Proverbs 29:12 (MSG)

9) Guard the reputation of yourself and your team.

A good leader casts a positive shadow and always tries to act ethically and morally and earn a good reputation. A true leader also works at building a good reputation for her team too. Pat Williams encouraged, "Whether you are a parent, teacher, coach or manager in business, your primary responsibility is to bring out the best in the people you lead."

Being a person of good moral character is essential to having a good reputation. Dwight L. Moody spoke to that when he said, "If I take care of my character, my reputation will take care of myself."

"A good and honest life is a blessed memorial; a wicked life leaves a rotten stench." — Proverbs 10:7 (MSG)

"A sterling reputation is better than striking it rich; a gracious spirit is better than money in the bank."— Proverbs 22:1 (MSG)

10) Be respectful to your boss and other leaders.

Effective leaders are respectful to their boss and other leaders they work with. The best leaders are also good followers. Aristotle advised, "All great leaders must first learn to follow." Likewise Sam Rayburn adds, "You cannot be a leader, and ask other people to follow you, unless you know how to follow too."

"A wise heart takes orders ..." — Proverbs 10:8 (MSG)

"Fear God, dear child–respect your leaders; don't be defiant or mutinous." — Proverbs 24:21-22 (MSG)

"Don't bad-mouth your leaders, not even under your breath, and don't abuse your betters, even in the privacy of your own home. Loose talk has a way of getting picked up and spread around. Little birds drop the crumbs of your gossip far and wide." — Ecclesiastes 10:20 (MSG)

11) Remain steady in times of stress and crisis.
The most respected leaders are those that don't panic when stress or a crisis hits. When something bad happens, the shadow of the leader will have a huge impact if people focus on the problem—or instead focus on the solution. Keeping calm, poised, and focusing on working together to resolve the challenge will go a long way to a successful resolution.

"When the country is in crisis, everybody has a plan to fix it – but it takes a leader of real understanding to straighten things out." — Proverbs 28:2 (MSG)

12) Be diligent and work hard.
Leaders that have strong work ethics get more done—and earn the respect of the people around them. When leaders are

diligent and work hard we set a positive example for our team members, and have credibility when we set expectations of hard work from them.

"Indolence wants it all and gets nothing; the energetic have something to show for their lives."   — Proverbs 13:4 (MSG)

"All hard work brings a profit ..."   — Proverbs 14:23 (NIV)

13) Make sure you have a strong moral foundation.

The most successful leaders over the long-term have a strong moral compass and well defined values. Roy E. Disney wisely said, "When your values are clear to you, making decision becomes easier." The Judeo-Christian values found in the Ten Commandments are a good starting place for us to consider.

"Good leaders abhor wrongdoing of all kinds. Sound leadership has a moral foundation."   — Proverbs 16:12 (MSG)

"Whoever goes hunting for what is right and kind finds life-glorious life!"   — Proverbs 21:21 (MSG)

14) Be a person of good character and high integrity who always speaks the truth.

Effective leaders are men and women of good character, who model and promote integrity within their organizations. Integrity builds trust; trust leads to deeper bonds with employees and customers. Roy Kroc asserted, "The quality of a leader is reflected in the standards they set for themselves."

The importance of good character for leaders was emphasized by General Norman Schwarzkopf when he said, "Ninety-nine percent of leadership failures are failures of character."

"The integrity of the honest keeps them on track; the deviousness of crooks brings them to ruin." — Proverbs 11:3 (MSG)

"We don't expect eloquence from fools, nor do we expect lies from our leaders." —   Proverbs 17:7 (MSG)

"A leader of good judgment gives stability; an exploiting leader leaves a trail of waste."   — Proverbs 29:4 (MSG)

15) Be self-controlled and manage your anger.

The lack of self-control and poor anger management has led to the downfall of many leaders. Anger is an emotion that we all feel at times; the key is to manage it well and express it appropriately.

I have found it helpful when I feel myself getting angry to take a "time out" to analyze what's stimulating the anger (remember our mother's advice to count to ten?). After calming myself down, I try to rationally get a healthy perspective on how to resolve peacefully, and then try and draw out what I can learn from the situation for future reference.

"Mean-tempered leaders are like mad dogs; the good-natured are like fresh morning dew."   — Proverbs 19:12 (MSG)

"A person without self-control is like a house with its doors and windows knocked out."   — Proverbs 25:28 (MSG)

"Hot tempers start fights; a calm, cool sprit keeps the peace."
— Proverbs 15:18(MSG)

16) Be humble, and be a "giver".

The most effective leaders have a sense of humility. Humility in leaders is attractive; arrogance is repulsive. Jim Collins in his research about the most successful organizations found that their leaders tended to be "level 5" leaders.

Level 5 leaders have a combination of personal humility and professional will. Modesty and courage elevate these leaders to the top of their organizations, while simultaneously contributing to their organization's success. Collins explains, "...their ambition is first and foremost for the institution, not themselves."

The most respected leaders are also givers, not takers. President Calvin Coolidge observed, "No person was ever honored for what he received. Honor has been the reward for what he gave."

"First pride, then the crash–the bigger the ego, the harder the fall." — Proverbs 16:18 (MSG)

"Pride lands you flat on your face; humility prepares you for honor." — Proverbs 29:23 (MSG)

"The world of the generous gets larger and larger; the world of the stingy gets smaller and smaller. The one who blesses others is abundantly blessed; those who help others are helped." — Proverbs 11:24-25 (MSG)

PART TWO:
MANAGEMENT LESSONS

"Management is the opportunity to help people become better people. Practiced that way, it's a magnificent profession."—Clayton Christiansen

"The secret to winning is constant, consistent management." —Tom Landry

10

The Best Practices of Great Managers

"In every business, in every industry, management does matter."
—**Michael Eisner**

B eing in a management role is a great privilege—and a great challenge! Effective management does not happen by accident. Great managers understand what's most important for them to do—then do it! Fortunately, we don't have to stumble in the dark about what the top managers do. We have research that can shed light for us.

Trying to improve our management capabilities is important to the success of our organizations. Many people in the human resource field are telling us that the number one challenge facing organizations in the years ahead is the ability to attract and retain talented employees. This is becoming more challenging due to the aging demographics facing our nation. The reality is that the large baby boomer generation is starting to retire and will continue to retire in the years ahead.

How do organizations succeed at attracting and retaining the talent they need to prosper? Studies tell us that talented employees want and need great managers. How long employees stay and how productive they are is primarily determined by the relationship with their immediate supervisor. The number one reason why talented people leave is because they have a poor relationship with their boss.

So how do we become better managers? One tool we have is to learn and apply what research tells us. The Gallup organization has been engaged in employee and management research for over 25 years, and has collected information from over one million employees and interviewed thousands of managers. Their studies have revealed to us what the world's top performing managers do, and it boils down to four major activities (best practices).

Four Key Best Practices of Great Managers

According to the research, the four key activities of great managers are:
1) Picking People: *Select for Talent*
2) Set Expectations: *Define the Right Outcomes*
3) Motivate People: *Focus on Strengths*
4) Develop People: *Find the Right Fit*

Picking People: Select for Talent

The first key activity involves picking people well, focusing around their talents. Talent has been defined as the "recurring pattern of thought, feeling, or behavior that can be productively applied". Skills can be learned, knowledge can be gained, but talent is more "hard wired" and tougher to teach.

One approach in looking for talented people for our teams is to only hire "ACEs". ACE is an acrostic where the "A" stands for

Attitude. Look for people that have a positive attitude and that are committed, teachable and care for people.

"C" stands for character. Does character count? As an employee of a company that has been owned by Enron, I would say an emphatic yes! Look for people that exhibit integrity, honesty and are trustworthy.

"E" stands for enthusiasm. Are apathy and cynicism contagious? Yes! Is enthusiasm contagious? Yes! What makes for stronger and more productive teams? The answer is obvious. Here is the bottom line. If you hire ACEs for your team (and help existing employees develop into ACEs) – your team will be successful!

Set Expectations: Define the Right Outcomes

The second key is to set expectations, which is to define the right outcomes. Great managers focus their people toward performance by defining the right outcomes. How do you define the right outcomes? The 360-degree approach is one wise strategy. Find out where your boss and the senior management want the organization to go, and then determine how your team can help them get there. Coordinate with your peers and find ways to partner. Solicit participation from your team members—their participation leads to their buy-in and better quality decisions.

Once the right outcomes are defined, great managers then let each person find his own route toward the outcomes, within specified parameters. Great managers don't micro-manage. But they do define steps to ensure quality, safety and compliance with corporate policies and applicable laws.

Great managers are aware of the concept of "stakeholder symmetry". Stakeholder symmetry recognizes that an organization has multiple stakeholders (e.g. investors, customers, employees, suppliers, community). The organization should try to add value to each stakeholder, and maintain a reasonable balance between their competing interests.

Motivate People: Focus on Strengths

The third key is to motivate people, in part by focusing on each person's strengths. Great managers focus and use people's strengths, and manage around their weaknesses. Avoid the tendency to try and "fix" people. Instead, do everything you can to help each person cultivate his talents and become more of what he already is.

Develop People: Find the Right Fit

The final key is to develop people, by helping find the right fit. Great managers steer employees toward roles where the employee has the greatest chance of success. Jim Collin's book "Good to Great" chronicles an intensive research effort that identified and analyzed the nation's top long-term performing companies. One of the characteristics of these exceptional performing companies is that they "got the right people on the bus, and the wrong people off it." In other words, the very top performing companies find the right people for the right roles, and then let these people determine strategy and use their talents.

One practical tool that may be helpful is the Strengths Interview (from the book *First, Break all the Rules* by Buckingham and Coffman, which is an excellent source of research results). You can use this with new members on your team, and you can use this annually with existing team members.

The Strengths Interview

1) What did you enjoy most about your previous work experience? What brought you here? (If an existing employee) What keeps you here?

2) What do you think your strengths are?

3) What about your weaknesses?

4) What are your goals for your current role?

5) How often do you like to meet with me to discuss your progress? Are you the kind of person who will tell me how you are feeling or will I have to ask?

6) Do you have any personal goals or commitment you would like to tell me about?

7) What is the best praise you ever received? What made it so good?

8) Have you had any really productive partnerships or mentors? Why do you think these relationships worked so well for you?

9) What are your future goals? Your career goals? Are there any particular skills you want to learn? Are there some specific challenges you want to experience? How can I help?

10) Is there anything else you want to talk about that might help us work well together?

Once you have determined that you have an employee who is a good fit for your team, there are some practical tools that can help you in the development process. Tools include cross-training, attendance at relevant conferences, reading of trade journals, involvement in trade organizations, university courses, local seminars—the list goes on.

None of us are perfect managers – but we can all get better. Good luck as you continue on your path to being a better manager!

11

Ten Habits of Highly Effective Managers

"Sow a thought and you reap an act; sow an act and you reap a habit; sow a habit and you reap a character; sow a character and you reap a destiny."
—Ralph Waldo Emerson

Right in the middle of the quotation above is the importance of our habits. A habit is "an acquired mode of behavior that has become our common practice." Our habits mold our character and ultimately determine our destiny in the world. Want to further develop your character and become a highly effective manager? Intentionally pursuing and building worthwhile habits is the key.   Following are ten of the habits of highly effective managers. This is not an exhaustive list, but these will build a strong foundation on your road to increased management effectiveness:

Habit #1: "Expanding Self-Awareness" Having a high level of Emotional Intelligence (EQ) is essential to being an effective Manager—and EQ starts with having accurate self-awareness. Self-awareness can help us gain self-control and be helpful to people around us, not hurtful. Some tools to help expand our self-awareness include: get feedback from others such as using 360-degree surveys; have a mentor to speak into your life; and constantly seek feedback from others on how we are doing.

Habit #2: "Pursue Continuous Learning and Continuous Improvement" Are you a perfect manager and person? Me neither! What we can do is to commit ourselves to be life-long learners and seek to continuously improve ourselves as managers and as human beings. I have been inspired by this quote from Dr. Martin Luther King: "I may not be the man I want to be; I may not be the man I ought to be; I may not be the man I can be; but praise God, I'm not the man I once was."

Habit #3: "Always do the Right Thing" Too many people have been victimized by the unethical behavior of those in leadership roles. Remember Enron? My co-workers and I at Portland General will never forget. We were owned by Enron at the time of their bankruptcy and our retirement savings were decimated. Mark Twain said, "Always do what is right. It will gratify half of mankind and astound the other." My former pastor Loren Fischer said "It's always right to do right," and I agree.

Habit #4: "Be Results *and* Relationship Oriented" As leaders we are expected to get results—and we should. At the same time, building positive relationships is the right thing to do, and it leads to great results. One tool to help build relationships is to consistently practice the **3 Rs** with people. **Recognize** people for who they are and what they do; **Reward** people for individual and team achievements; and show people **Respect**. Everybody wants to be respected, as the classic Aretha Franklin song emphasizes.

Habit #5: "Achieve Big Goals one small step at a time "I remember a grade school friend telling me the following riddle: "Question: how do you eat an elephant? Answer: one bite at a time." Get the point? We need to set long-term visions and big goals for ourselves and our teams. And we need to break down the journey towards the vision and goals into manageable steps that inspire others to move forward.

Habit #6: "See the glass as half-full" Are you normally a pessimist or an optimist? Studies have shown that the most effective leaders are strong optimists. Being optimistic does not mean that we ignore the half of the glass that is empty. It does mean we are thankful for the half that is full, and we work together to fill the rest of the glass as best we can.

Habit #7: "Look for the win-win" Effective managers don't get locked into specific positions, but look for ways to meet interests of themselves and others so everybody gets something (a "win-win" versus a "win-lose").

Habit #8: "Spend much time in Quadrant 2" Stephen Covey popularized the importance of intentionally spending significant time doing "Important, Not Urgent" items. These include things like building relationships, reading and other learning activities, planning and thinking, exercise, etc. To spend more time in Quadrant 2, we need to spend less time in Quadrants 3 & 4 (i.e. "Urgent, Not Important" and "Not Urgent, Not Important") activities like watching TV, playing video games and wasting time doing things that add no value to our lives or the lives of others.

Habit #9: "Enjoy the journey" Management (and life!) is a journey filled with both positive and negative experiences. The journey will be much more pleasant and we will go farther if we learn to laugh and be thankful. A Yiddish proverb says, "What soap is to the body, laughter is to the soul." Studies have shown that laughter makes us physically and emotionally healthier, and more fun to be around too. Find a funny friend; enjoy a funny TV show or movie, and just laugh! Being thankful is also important. The reality is that we all have much to be thankful for, and our lives will be more joyful and productive if we learn to develop an "attitude of gratitude".

Habit #10: "Remember, your health is your wealth" Gandhi said, "It is health that is real wealth and not pieces of gold and silver." Living a healthy lifestyle will increase your energy, stamina and emotional well-being, and help you be more effective in all you do. A holistic, healthy lifestyle includes developing and using our mental capabilities (read a good book lately or taken a class just for the learning?). We are also spiritual beings, and finding faith and serving others can nourish our spiritual health.

Let me leave you with a challenge to not settle for mediocrity, but to get in the game and go for management excellence. Listen to this President Teddy Roosevelt quote. "It is not the critic who counts, nor the man who points out how the strong man stumbles, or where the doers of deeds could have done them better. The credit belongs to the man who is actually in the arena, whose face is marred by dust and sweat and blood; who strives valiantly ... who spends himself in a worthy cause."

12

Is Your Team High Performing or Hardly Performing?

"Teamwork is the fuel that allows common people
to attain uncommon results."
—Andrew Carnegie

According to a recent Gallup survey 69 percent of the United States work force is not fully engaged on the job.[1] Many work teams struggle and perform at a mediocre level—or worse. In contrast, some teams stand above the normal and are high performance. These high performing teams (HPTs) are known for their positive morale, high motivation, productivity and commitment to excellence. How are HPTs developed and maintained?

An extensive research project involving over 2.5 million people in 237 companies sought to find out the common characteristics of HPTs.[2] It was discovered that HPTs share three characteristics that directly speak to the meeting of three important needs of team members. Let's take a look at these three keys to developing HPTs:

Keys to Developing High Performance Teams

Key #1: Sense of Fairness

HPTs are first of all characterized by a *sense of fairness*. People have a need to be treated equitably, and that sense of fairness has three components. There is a *physical component*—this includes a safe working environment, realistic workload, and reasonably comfortable working conditions.

Another component is *economic fairness*. People have a need to feel they are paid a fair day's pay for a fair day's work, with satisfactory benefits, and have a reasonable degree of job security.

The third component is *equity*—being treated respectfully. Included is a reasonable accommodation for personal and family needs and being treated like an adult, not a child.

One way to monitor the perception of fairness on your team is to conduct an annual team survey – and include some questions related to fairness.

Key #2: Sense of Achievement

HPTs are characterized by a *sense of achievement*. Achievement includes taking pride in one's accomplishments by doing things that matter and doing them well; receiving recognition for one's accomplishments; and taking pride in the organization's accomplishments.

There are six primary sources for a sense of achievement:

1) Challenge of the work itself
2) Acquiring new skills
3) Ability to perform
4) Perceived importance of employee's job
5) Recognition received for performance

6) Working for a company of which the employee can be proud

One tool we can use to help build a sense of achievement is to participatively set, and work together to achieve SMART goals. SMART goals are team goals that have these characteristics:

Specific

Measurable

Ambitious yet achievable

Results oriented

Time specific

Communicating progress and celebrating progress on goals will help develop a strong sense of achievement within your team.

Key #3: Sense of Camaraderie

Benjamin Franklin said, "We must indeed all hang together, or most assuredly, we shall all hang separately."

HPTs are characterized by a *sense of camaraderie* — having warm, positive and cooperative relations with others in the workplace ("one for all and all for one"). Setting, and then working together to achieve SMART goals helps build camaraderie. In addition, try having periodic fun and team-building activities. Need some ideas? Here is a list of five to get you thinking:

1) Take your team to a movie (the large screen IMAX movies are great — even better if in 3D!)

2) Play a fun game together, like your own customized version of "Family Feud".

3) Try a fun recreational activity like miniature golf, or just have an afternoon in the park.

4) Attend a favorite sporting event, concert or other social event that team members would enjoy (important to know your team on this one).

5) Last but not least, anything with FOOD seems to be a big hit. Either having food catered in or going out to a nearby restaurant seems to always be appreciated.

A tremendous yet overlooked tool that leaders can use to help build camaraderie is recognition. To help carry out recognition well, consider these five recognition principles:

1) Be specific about what is being recognized.

2) Do it in person.

3) Be timely.

4) Be sincere.

5) Recognition should be given for both individual and group performance.

Putting it All Together

Let's look at the six things managers can do to maintain engagement with their employees on an on-going basis:

1) **Don't let the newbies sink**. Get your new employees off to a great start by clearly explaining the goals and expectations of the team, regularly checking in with them, and assigning a teammate as a "buddy" mentor.

2) **Create a physically comfortable work environment**. Ideas can come from peers, conferences and the employees themselves.

3) **Eliminate perks that favor one level of employee over another**. Goal is to avoid sending the message that some

employees are "second class", when in reality everybody contributes to the success of the team.

4) **Avoid micro managing**. Give employees as much flexibility and as many choices as you can. Avoid "dirty delegation" and think about how you would like to be treated.

5) **Spill the beans**. If we don't communicate a vacuum is created. The vacuum is filled with the rumor mill, which is notoriously negative and will sink morale faster than the iceberg sunk the Titanic.

6) **Observe basic courtesies**. Never underestimate the value of simple greetings, a smile, or saying thank you. These courtesies send a positive message to employees that they are appreciated and you care.

Let me leave you with a quote from Fred Smith, CEO of Federal Express: "The way I see it, leadership does not begin with power but rather with a compelling vision and a goal of excellence." I wish you well as you intentionally pursue the development of even higher levels of team performance!

13

Recognition: The Missing Ingredient to Great Results

**"People work for money, but go the extra mile
for recognition, praise and rewards."**
—Dale Carnegie

W ant to be a more effective manager? One key is to develop an
environment where your team members can be motivated to
excel. The secret to developing a motivating work environment is
the use of positive consequences such as recognition.

Research over the years has led to the development of what some
have called the "Greatest Management Principle in the World" *You
get what you reward.* Sincere, regular and positive recognition and
rewarding of desired behaviors is common sense—but not common
practice. A Gallup poll of thousands of employees found that 65 percent claimed to have received no praise or recognition the past year!

Everyone likes to be recognized and shown appreciation. William
James was one of the most respected psychologists who ever lived.
After a lifetime of research and practice he concluded that most

people's greatest need is the need for *appreciation*. On-going recognition and praise makes a person feel appreciated, important, and stimulates the intrinsic motivation to excel.

Gallup research found that individuals who receive regular recognition and praise:

- increase their individual productivity
- increase engagement among their colleagues
- are more likely to stay with their organization
- receive higher loyalty and satisfaction scores from customers
- have better safety records and fewer accidents on the job

On the other hand, a survey by Robert Half Associates showed that the number one reason for leaving a company was "limited recognition and praise".

There are specific actions we can take to improve our recognition practices. Following are the "Top Ten Ways to Motivate Employees" (adapted from recognition expert Bob Nelson's book entitled *Motivating Today's Employees*):

1) **Provide Personal Thanks**. Mark Twain said that he could " ... go two months on just one compliment." JRR Tolkien was quoted as saying, "Kind words cost little, but are worth much." A landmark research study showed the number one thing that employees wanted was "full appreciation for work done".

2) **Make Time for Employees.** What kind of message do we send when we meet with and listen to employees? That we care. John Maxwell captures the importance when he says, "People don't care how much we know, until they know how much we care."

3) **Provide Specific Feedback**. Employees want to know how they are personally doing, and how the department and organization are doing. Also, catch people doing things right and thank them!

4) **Create an Open (and fun) Environment**. Having an open, fun and trusting environment helps build a sense of camaraderie and encourages new ideas and innovation.

5) **Provide Information**. I agree with Carla O'Dell when she stated, "If you don't give people information, they'll make up something to fill the void." The void that is created gets filled by the "rumor mill". This is invariably negative. Nitin Nohria wisely stated, "Communication is the real work of leadership."

6) **Involve Employees in Decisions**. Involving employees in decisions that impact them results in buy-in, as well as better quality decisions.

7) **Reward High Performers**. Promoting and rewarding people based on their performance (not politics) sends the right signals. Also, dealing with poor performers so they improve or leave strengthens the team and really helps morale.

8) **Develop a Sense of Ownership.** Provide employees a sense of ownership in their work and in their work environment.

9) **Give Chances to Grow and Learn**. Most employees desire to grow and learn. Helping them recognizes their contributions and potential.

10) **Celebrate Successes.** Taking the time to celebrate the successes of individuals, the team and the organization builds morale and the motivation to strive for future successes.

Many of us have good intentions to show more recognition, but often fall short. Here are a few ideas to help build recognition into our regular routines:

Use a "To-Do" List or Daily Planner. At the beginning of the week, write down the names of your team members and others you intend to recognize during the week ahead. Catch someone doing something right, recognize them, and then mark your list. On your planner you can record birthdays, anniversary dates with the company, etc.

Use E-Mail and/or Voicemail. Send positive, personal messages to let someone know you appreciate their work. At the end of the day, leave a positive voice mail thanking them for their excellent work that day, and express appreciation for them being on your team. I guarantee when they come to work the next morning, and that's the first thing they hear, they will have a great day!

Use Thank You notes. Have a stack of notes readily available. Send hand written notes on a regular basis. One manager told me she has a standing appointment for one hour on Friday afternoons that she uses to write notes and do other forms of recognition.

Let me close with a quote from Saint Paul: "Give everyone what you owe him … if respect, then respect; if honor then honor" (Romans 13:7). Good luck to you as recognize your employees and let them know how much you appreciate them!

14

How Do You Motivate People?

"Management is nothing more than motivating other people."
—Lee Iacocca

Motivation is an important key to sustained individual and team performance—perhaps the top key! Can we directly motivate another person? Not really—but we can intentionally foster a climate that helps people motivate themselves. President Dwight D. Eisenhower said it well, "Motivation is the art of getting people to do what you want them to do because **they** want to do it."

The secret to effective motivation is to promote *intrinsic* motivation—that internal motivation people can have to perform well for psychological reasons that go beyond external rewards. Modern day motivational expert Daniel Pink asserts that, "Intrinsically motivated employees find more personal satisfaction in their work, and are consistently more motivated, with less prodding and cajoling from management."

How do we intrinsically motivate employees? We can get some guidance by reviewing the findings of the classic motivation research of Dr. Frederick Herzberg and validated by numerous studies since then. Let's review the basic findings of Herzberg's "Two-Factor Motivational Model".

Two-Factor Motivational Model: Satisfiers versus Dissatisfiers

Herzberg and other researchers have found that work environments contain "hygiene" factors that, if not done well, lead to job dissatisfaction (i.e. are "dissatisfiers"). Two key points are 1) not doing well on these hygiene factors will contribute to job dissatisfaction and 2) doing well on these factors will NOT lead to job satisfaction, but will keep motivation neutral. The primary hygiene (dissatisfiers) are:

1) Company policy and administration
2) Supervision
3) Relationship with supervisor
4) Work conditions
5) Salary

The key here is to participatively engage with employees and develop policies, practices and work conditions that are viewed as fair and positive. By itself you will not be contributing much to the satisfaction and motivation of your employees. But you will avoid fueling dissatisfaction and demotivating them.

Satisfiers (Motivators)

Herzberg and other researchers have also discovered a set of factors that are considered "satisfiers" or "motivators". Assuming the hygiene factors are being satisfactorily met, these factors are what truly inspire and motivate employees. And these factors have a strong "intrinsic" bent to them—they speak to our heart-felt psychological needs and can be intrinsic to the job. There are six major motivators:

1) **Achievement:** employees need to have a sense of achievement, believing that they are accomplishing something that matters.

2) **Recognition:** people desire to be appreciated and recognized by their bosses and others for their contributions.

3) **Work Itself:** the work should be meaningful, interesting and challenging for the employee to perform and feel motivated.

4) **Responsibility:** The employee must hold themselves responsible for the work. The supervisors should give them ownership of the work, and minimize control but retain accountability.

5) **Advancement:** Employees should feel that by excelling in their current work, they have the opportunity to advance in responsibilities and into other positions that they find appealing.

6) **Growth:** Employees should feel they have opportunities to grow their skills and develop as value-added members of the organization.

External rewards do have their place and can help motivate under some circumstances. But what is interesting about the above list is these are not external-reward driven, but involve intrinsic elements that can be cultivated by intentional job enrichment and motivational management practices.

All generations in the work force desire and can be inspired by these intrinsic motivators, especially the younger generation. For example, I am a baby boomer who has been with the same company from the day I graduated from college years ago. In contrast, my oldest daughter left her first job after working there less than a year— and took a small pay cut! Why? She wanted to work someplace where the motivators above were more evident. She worked at her second job for years and really liked it!

Principles for Putting Satisfiers (Motivators) Into Practice

Principle:	Motivators Involved:
Remove some controls while retaining accountability.	Responsibility & Achievement
Increase the accountability of individuals for their own work.	Responsibility & Recognition
Greater personal responsibility for quality of work, less scrutiny by supervisors.	Responsibility & Recognition
Giving a person a complete natural unit of work (e.g. let employees sign a letter they produced or present a report they prepared).	Responsibility, Achievement & Recognition
Granting additional authority to employees; job freedom.	Responsibility, Achievement & Recognition
Sharing some reports and information directly with workers rather than through the supervisors.	Internal Recognition
Introducing new and more difficult tasks not previously handled.	Growth & Learning
Assign individuals specific or specialized tasks, enabling them to become experts.	Responsibility, Growth & Advancement
Bring employees to some meetings; give employees credit for their work that goes to people outside the team.	Recognition, Growth
Give a person opportunity to lead special projects and assignments.	Recognition, Growth, Advancement

The key to applying the satisfiers is to *enrich* jobs to make them psychologically appealing and inspiring. Following is a table of principles to help us enrich jobs:

Let me close with a quote from Homer Rice: "You can motivate by fear and you can motivate by reward. But both of these methods are only temporary. The only lasting thing is self-motivation."

I wish you well in your pursuit of creating a motivating work environment that will inspire your employees and lead to great performance and results for your team!

15

Developing Your People: the Key to a Successful Team

"The only thing worse than training employees and losing them, is not training them and keeping them."
—Zig Ziglar

Dale Galloway stated, "The growth and development of people is the highest calling of a leader." Developing people is crucial to the success of our teams.

HR experts make a distinction between *training* (improving people's skills in their current job) and *development* (improving skills for future roles). Both training and development are essential and can be inter-related. We train and develop our people though a two-step process:

1) Education: learning what to do
2) Application: doing what you learned

Following are 15 specific tools we can use to train and develop our people:

1. College/University Classes

As a long-time university instructor I can attest to the value of having your people take classes to broaden their knowledge and sharpen their basic skills. Whether a person is degree oriented or not, taking classes in management, operations, human resources, finance, information technology, etc. provides an educational foundation that enhances a person's ability to excel at doing real work back at the work place.

2. In-House Classes

Larger companies often have in-house classes available on a variety of useful topics. Work with your Human Resource folks. Don't be bashful in suggesting classes that would be of value to people on your team and throughout the organization.

3. External Seminars & Webinars

There are a number of companies (e.g. Fred Pryor, Career Track, Skill Path, AMA) that offer one or two day seminars on useful topics ranging from working with vendors, to time management to dealing with difficult employees. There is also an increasing number of free or low-cost webinars available covering a wide range of topics. I build in dollars in my budget to cover some classes for employees and I urge you to do so too.

4. Conferences

Participating in relevant conferences (like National Postal Forum and MAILCOM in the Mail profession or Credit Congress in the credit profession) is a great investment and has many benefits. I am actively involved in conferences and get some of my people involved because nothing matches the opportunities at a good conference: ability to learn best practices from the top leaders and practitioners in the industry; ability to learn and see in action the latest technology; ability to network with peers, vendors and industry experts; and the stimulation to go back home and move your operation to a higher level of excellence. Some may say they can't afford to attend a conference. I would say how can you afford not to?

5. Trade and Professional Associations

I belong to several associations and encourage you to do likewise—and have some of your team members join you. Trade associations provide opportunities for learning, networking and professional development. Volunteering to serve in your local chapter further enhances the benefits to you and your organization by deeper networking and leadership development.

6. Professional Certification Programs

Pursuing certification programs is a great way to challenge yourself and deepen your understanding of the field. My supervisors over the years have earned multiple certifications among them, and the majority of the Printing & Mail Services department is certified. Key certifications related to the mail industry are the "Certified Mail Systems Distribution Manager" and "Mail Piece Design Consultant" (refer to msmanational.org) and the "Executive Mail Center Manager" and "Mail Piece Design Professional" (see usps.com).

7. Recurring Team Meetings

Many teams meet on a periodic basis for information sharing purposes. There is also an opportunity to add an education component to some of these recurring meetings. You or your team members can report out on learning from conferences and local trade association events. You can invite subject matter experts from other parts of your company to do presentations. I have used leaders and experts from Finance, HR, Customer Service, and various operational areas to help educate us. Training videos are also a great resource for team meetings.

8. Off-site training days

For concentrated learning, taking people away from the work site for a one-half or full day training session is unbeatable. I have off-site training for entire teams that often focuses on team building skills in additional to technical training. We have quarterly off-site meetings for my Supervisors and Leads that focus on leadership and management training.

9. Trade Journals

Trade journals are a great tool to keep up with current developments in the industry and learn best practices from industry experts. For anybody in the mail industry, I recommend Mail Journal (www. mailomg.com) and Mailing Systems and Technology (mailingsystemsmag.com).

10. Job Shadowing

Job shadowing involves having a person spend a period of time (often one to eight hours) "shadowing" another to better understand what that person does. I have used job shadowing to allow potential Supervisors or Managers to shadow myself or one of my Supervisors to gain a feel for what is expected. Team members have shadowed others in connecting departments to broaden their understanding of the interfaces between departments.

11. Mentoring

Serving as a "mentor" or participating as a "mentoree" is educational and valuable. I spent five years as a "mentoree" with a Vice President of the company. I learned a lot from the experience and had a good sounding board when facing challenges on my teams. Likewise, I have served as a mentor to a number of employees within the company in recent years, and really have enjoyed their opportunity to help develop people and to support mutual learning.

12. Special Projects & Assignments; Give Presentations

Giving people a chance to work on special projects is a great method to learn new skills and apply "book learning". I will intentionally give team members projects to lead or support as opportunities to help them gain hands on experience and build their practical expertise.

13. On Job Training

It's been said that nothing beats OJT (On Job Training) for skill development. Providing OJT by supervisors or experienced teammates helps people understand and perform the tasks they need to be successful.

14. Cross Training

Cross training provides people a chance to develop new skills and expertise and gain new experiences that stimulate professional growth.

15. Non-profit Volunteering

The late management guru Peter Drucker was a big proponent for volunteering in non-profit organizations. Volunteerism is a classic "win-win". The non-profits gain value from the volunteers, and the volunteers also benefit. Benefits to volunteers include the chance to network with people outside the company, chance to use and sharpen existing skills, and the opportunity to develop leadership abilities by actively working with others to help the non-profit pursue its mission of serving its communities.

Seeing people grow personally and professionally is very rewarding. I wish you the best as you work to develop your people!

16

Does Your Team Work?

"Alone we can do so little; together we can do so much."
—Helen Keller

For us fans of team sports, isn't it exciting to see our favorite teams blend together their individual talents and abilities and achieve success as a unified team? The good news is that our teams in the business world can also achieve success—and a key to make that happen is **teamwork**.

What is teamwork? I like Andrew Carnegie's definition: "Teamwork is the ability to work together toward a common vision. The ability to direct individual accomplishments toward organizational objectives. *It is the fuel that allows common people to attain uncommon results."* How can we develop stronger teamwork? Let me share Ten Principles of High Performance teamwork that I think can be helpful.[1]

Ten Principles to Build High Performance Teamwork

1) **Build Trust with Integrity.** As a leader of a team, we need to walk with integrity and build trust for us, as well as among all team members. Building trust comes down to being a person of good character. Marsha Sinetar said it well: "Trust is not a matter of technique, but of character. We are trusted because of our way of being, not because of our polished exteriors or our expertly crafted communications." We model integrity and build trust as we walk or talk, listen to others, always be honest, and be humble enough to admit our mistakes and ask for forgiveness when needed.

2) **Put the Team First.** In the middle of every high performance team is a common purpose: a sense of vision and mission that unites and inspires each individual team member. Make sure you solicit participation from the team when developing the common purpose. Remember the principle that "change imposed is change opposed", and Ken Blanchard's quote that "None of us is as smart as all of us." Alexander Graham Bell summarized well when he said, "All winning teams are goal oriented. Teams like these win consistently because everyone connected with them concentrates on specific objectives. They go about their business with blinders on: nothing will distract them from achieving their aims."

3) **Communicate Openly and Candidly.** High performing teams are empowered teams, and information is a great source of power. Sharing the team's key performance metrics and indicators and on-going status is crucial. Ask yourself, "What do team members need to know on a daily, weekly and monthly basis to manage performance?" Tools such as

balanced scorecards, dashboards, team work review meetings and 1-on-1 coaching sessions can be helpful.

4) **Be Part of the Solution, Not the Problem.** There is no substitute for personal ownership, responsibility and self-control. These are traits that we can model — and intentionally encourage in our team members. Also, recognize that problems will arise. They may be blessings in disguise if we learn and grow from them. Mark Victor Hansen encourages us: "Problems are good, not bad. Welcome them and they become the solution. Rene Descartes adds: "Each problem that I solved became a rule which served afterwards to solve other problems."

5) **Commit to Excellence.** One of my sayings is that, "We can choose to be mediocre, or we can choose to strive for excellence. The choice is ours." The reality is that if we don't *intentionally* choose to strive for excellence the default choice is to settle for being mediocre. I resonate with Mario Andretti when he says, "Desire is the key to motivation, but its determination and commitment to an unrelenting pursuit of your goal — *a commitment to excellence* — that will enable you to attain the success you seek."

6) **Promote an Atmosphere of Respect.** One way to show we really respect someone is to actively listen to them and then respond appropriately. Socrates once stated, "You have two ears and one mouth. Use them appropriately." James O'Toole explained a benefit of active listening when he said, "Almost all employees, if they see that they will be listened to, and they have adequate information, will be able to find ways to

improve their own performance and the performance of their work group."

Showing respect also includes positive encouragement and expressing our appreciation and approval. I like Charles Schwab's quote, "I have never seen a man who could do real work except under the stimulus of *encouragement* and enthusiasm and the *approval* of the people for whom he was working."

7) **Ask and Encourage the Right Questions.** The art of questioning is an important management skill. It is a "pulling" technique—challenging people to think, to probe, to investigate, to challenge assumptions and to seek answers. John Chancellor illustrated the importance of this skill. "If you take a close look at the most successful people in life, you'll find that their strength is not in having the right answers, but in asking the right questions."

8) **Use a Rational Problem-Solving Process.** Albert Einstein supported the need for rational and thoughtful problem solving processes when he said, "The significant problems we face cannot be solved at the same level of thinking we were at when we created them."

There are a number of rational problem solving processes to choose from. One such approach is to follow these steps:

1. Gather data
2. Review facts
3. Define the problem and desired end-state
4. Ask questions and identify alternative solutions
5. Evaluate each alternative

6. Select "best" alternative

7. Implement chosen alternative

8. Evaluate after-the-fact effectiveness of solution; make changes if necessary

9) **Promote Interdependent Thinking**. The key here is to promote "we" thinking—not "me" thinking. Vince Lombardi encourages us: "Build for your team a feeling of oneness, of dependence on one another and of strength to be derived by unity." Having talented team members and encouraging development of individuals is important, but Michael Jordan puts it into perspective with, "Talent wins games, but *teamwork* and intelligence win championships." Phil Jackson adds, "The strength of the team is each individual member. The strength of each member is the team."

10) **Pull the Weeds.** Most people on a team are willing and able to "play by the rules" and be a value added member of a successful team. But in reality, sometimes we may have a team member that is either not capable or not willing to meet expectations—even after we have tried to remedy the situation. We are then faced with the choice of allowing the "weed" to remain and hold back the team's success, or to remove the weed so the rest of the team can grow. Voltaire said, "we must cultivate our garden," and that applies to the teams we lead.

Let me close with a quote from soccer great Mia Hamm: "I am a member of a team, and I rely on the team. I defer to it and sacrifice for it, because the team, not the individual, is the ultimate champion." Good luck as you intentionally work with your team to develop stronger teamwork and pursue an even higher level of success!

17

Creating a Great Workplace

"The most valuable "currency" of any organization is the initiative and creativity of its members. Every leader has the solemn moral responsibility to develop these to the maximum in all his people. This is the leader's highest priority."
—W. Edwards Deming

An organization will only achieve its full potential when people are engaged and inspired to do their best work. Research from the Hay Group finds that highly engaged employees on average are 50 percent more likely to exceed expectations than the least engaged workers. Companies with highly engaged people outperform organizations with the most disengaged workers by 54 percent in employee retention, 89 percent in customer satisfaction, and also in revenue growth.[1]

How do we create great workplaces that maximize our employees' engagement and potential, and the potential of the larger organization? A recent research project by professors Rob Goffee and Gareth

Jones identified six imperatives that the best work places possess. Let's look at these keys to successfully building a better workplace.

Keys to Building a Great Workplace

Here are the six key imperatives to creating great workplaces:

1) **Individual differences are nurtured** ("you can be yourself"). Desmond Tutu stated, "Isn't it amazing that we were all made in God's image, yet there is so much diversity among his people?" The organizations with the best workplaces recognize and appreciate differences in the traditional diversity categories (race, religion, gender, age, etc.). However they don't stop there. These organizations also honor and provide room for differences in style, perspective, thinking and core assumptions.

    Malcom Forbes spoke to this philosophy when he said, "Diversity is the art of thinking independently *together*." To evaluate how well your particular team is doing, consider asking team members questions like, "Do you feel comfortable being yourself at work?" and, "Are we all encouraged to express our opinions?"

2) **Information is not suppressed or spun** ("you are told what is really going on"). The organizations doing well in this area do not deceive, stonewall, distort or spin. They realize that in today's real-time social media world you are better off telling people the truth before someone else does. Nobody likes to share bad news – but employees appreciate the truth and especially want to hear from their direct boss. Being transparent breeds trust – and trust leads to engagement and higher performance.

3) **The organization adds value to employees, rather than merely extracting it from them** ("your strengths are magnified"). The best organizations make it a priority to make their people better. They resonate with Bill Bradley when he said, "Leadership is unlocking people's potential to become better." Part of adding value includes helping employees improve in areas of weaknesses that impair success of the individual and the organization.

   But the best organizations focus on maximizing people's strengths. The importance of developing strengths is illustrated by Donald Clifton (co-author of *Now, Discover Your Strengths*) when he shared "Two key points: 1. Each person's talents are enduring and unique and 2. Each person's greatest room for growth is in the area of his or her greatest strength."

   You can evaluate how your team is doing by asking questions of your employees like "Am I being given the chance to develop?" and "Do you have a specific development plan?"

4) **The organization stands for something meaningful** ("stand for more than shareholder value"). People want to be a part of something bigger than themselves, something they can believe in. Leaders of the organizations that excel in this imperative take to heart Jack Welch's admonishment that, "A leader's job is to look into the future and see the organization, not at is, but as it should be." One practical tool to help develop greater meaning for an organization is to pursue "stakeholder symmetry"—this involves trying to add value to all major stakeholder groups and to balance out the interests of the stakeholders and look for the "win-wins".

Who are the key stakeholders to focus on? Some organizations have focused almost exclusively on the shareholders—and certainly they are one of the key stakeholders. But too much emphasis on shareholders will lead to problems with the other stakeholders and will not inspire employees and give them a sense of meaning. To inspire and give meaning also emphasize the key stakeholders of Customers, Employees and the Community. Focusing on providing great customer service, developing and treating your employees well and giving back to the community will really provide the bigger meaning that employees crave.

5) **The work itself is intrinsically rewarding** ("your daily work is rewarding and makes sense"). When it comes to work, President Theodore Roosevelt hit the mark when he said, "Far and away the best prize life has to offer is the chance to work hard at work worth doing." To make sure work is worth doing, we need to ask questions about the tasks each person is performing such as "Do those duties make sense? Why are they what they are? Are they as engaging as they can be?" Talking with the employees doing the work is crucial.

Also, we should look externally for better ways to accomplish the work – through professional organizations, conferences and trade journals!

6) **There are no stupid rules** ("have rules people can believe in"). Some rules are absolutely necessary. But sometimes organizations have arbitrary and unnecessary restrictions that frustrate employees. It's good to keep in mind President Franklin D. Roosevelt's quote that "Rules are not necessarily sacred, principles are." And we want to avoid stupid rules that

spark the sentiment that General Douglas McArthur shared when he said, "Rules are mostly made to be broken and are too often for the lazy to hide behind."

To evaluate how your employees feel about the rules you have in place, consider asking questions like "Are the rules clear and applied to everyone" and "Are there any unnecessary rules you think we can eliminate?"

Trying to improve in these six areas is not easy and is partially outside of our control. But certainly we can identify some specific strategies to help us improve in some of the areas where we fall short of our aspirations. More power to you as you strive to create an even more engaging and inspiring workplace!

18

The Power of Engagement

"People come to work wanting to be productive for the most part, and managers either set them up for success or cause confusion."
– Jim Harter, Chief Scientist and Engagement Expert at Gallup

One of the hot topics in the Human Resources field in recent years is employee engagement. Engagement is the level of discretionary effort exhibited by employee. Wikipedia defines an "engaged employee" as "one who is fully absorbed and enthusiastic about their work and so takes positive action to further the organization's reputation and interest". I want engaged employees on my teams – what about you? Let's talk about why engagement is important then we will explore some ways to try and improve engagement.

Why Is Employee Engagement Important?

A recent Gallup study showed only 31 percent of employees are actively engaged on the job.[1] Why should we care about the level of engagement? Because *there is a strong correlation between employee engagement and a number of important performance metrics*. For example–Gallup research showed that work units in the top quartile in employee engagement outperformed the bottom quartile units by: [1]

10 percent in Customer Ratings

22 percent in Profitability

21 percent in Productivity

25 percent lower turnover

37 percent less absenteeism

48 percent fewer safety incidents

41 percent less quality defects

Foundational Principles for Improving Engagement

In a recent article in *Talent Management,* Jim Harter from Gallup shared some key principles for increasing engagements based on Gallup's research:

1) **Engaged employees need to know what's expected of them at work – role clarity**. Only about half of employees say they know what's expected of them at work. This is considered the starting place for building greater engagement.

2) **Engaged employees have what they need to do the work.** This includes things like adequate procedures, tools, and support from others in the organization when needed (e.g. trainers, supervisors, staff support like IT and HR).

3) **Engaged employees are in jobs where that can utilize their talents effectively.** It's incumbent on us in management to understand our employee talents and strengths and to place people in roles that can excel at.

4) **Engaged employees receive recognition for good work in a way that's important for them as an individual.** Regular recognition is extremely important – and we also want to

try and recognize individuals in ways that are most meaningful to them.

The Seven Key Needs of Employees

One approach to increase engagement is to better understand the needs of each of your team members – then respond in ways that are meaningful to him/her. The American Management Association cites research that 99 percent of employees are motivated by one of the following seven needs:

1) **The Need for Achievement.** There are some us that are very motivated by the possibility of achievement. For us, identifying goals to strive for and then celebrating successes along the way is important for our desire to achieve and will motivate us to strive for even greater achievements. Here is a great litmus test to see if you have a very high need for achievement: if you use a "to-do" list and sometimes write down a recently completed task so that you have the pleasure of crossing it off – you are a high achiever!

2) **The Need for Power.** Some people have a need for power/control. These are the team members that can excel and be motivated by leading special projects or developing policy/procedure manuals or any other task where they have power, control or significant influence. Placing them in a role of power or control will be highly engaging for them and can benefit the entire team.

3) **The Need for Affiliation.** Some of our team members have a strong need for affiliation – to feel part of a larger team. These are great folks to help organize team building activities and to check in regularly to get a pulse on how the team is feeling.

4) **The Need for Autonomy.** We have team members that really like to have flexibility in their jobs and to be left alone to do them. These are folks that don't want public attention, but want the freedom to do their jobs with minimal outside influence. Finding jobs and tasks that allow for more autonomy is the obvious key to maximize the engagement of these team members.

5) **The Need for Esteem.** Some people have extra need to receive esteem. I remember awhile back I had a Supervisor that started working for me that I sensed was not as engaged and connecting with me as I thought was possible. I eventually figured out the best way to engage her was to provide extra "atta girls" via e-mail and face-to-face and help meet her need to feel esteemed.

6) **The Need for Safety and Security.** There are people that have an above average need to feel safe and secure. In today's ever changing corporate environments that we live in this can be challenging to meet that need. But we can address concerns as they arise, and provide realistic hope and accentuate the positive when helping those that struggle with feeling safe and secure.

7) **The Need for Equity.** Some team members have a strong need to feel that equity and fairness exists within the team and organization. It's good to have at least one person on the team that we can use as a barometer on how we are doing as managers to have equity and fairness in our work environment.

Proven Approaches for Engaging Employees

I recently ran across an article by Donna Fluss in *Connections Magazine* where she shared a dozen approaches that can help engage employees. I liked her list and wanted to share with you:

1) **Listen to Your Employees.** Invite employees to share their ideas and really listen to what they have to say. Act upon the ideas that are doable and make business sense.

2) **Involve Them.** Goal is to create an environment that welcomes innovative ideas and actions.

3) **Support them.** Be there for your employees – and treat them like adults (not children) and treat like valued family members.

4) **Excite them.** Communicate your department's direction and plans to your employees. Be the upfront cheerleader and help them see the positive opportunities that the future holds.

5) **Invest in them.** Our employees are truly our most important assets so let's invest our time and other resources in them.

6) **Develop them.** Give employees opportunities to develop in their current roles and help them be prepared for future roles.

7) **Challenge them**. Give employees new opportunities and help them grow to the next level.

8) **Recognize them.** Recognize both team and individual performance.

9) **Celebrate them.** Celebrate successes and strive to create a fun and positive work environment that makes it enjoyable to come to work.

10) **Respect them**. We all like to be respected, and to be respected by your boss is very motivating.

11) **Compensate them.** Pay people for a job well done as best as you can.

12) **Promote them**. Whenever possible, promoting from within will be motivating and shows that there are opportunities and that good performance is appreciated and rewarded.

The level of employee engagement on our teams can be positively influenced by those of us in management roles. It takes intentional effort to increase engagement levels – but the benefits are worth the effort. I wish you success in striving to better tap into the power of engagement!

19

Happiness: the Fuel to Success and Performance

"When we create happiness and positivity in the present, we're better at making a better world for other people afterwards."
- Dr. Shawn Anchor, author of *The Happiness Advantage*

Want to provide the fuel to drive your team to higher levels of success and performance? The fuel is **happiness**. Ground breaking research in the fields of positive psychology and neuroscience has shown that happiness is the precursor to success – not merely the result. And happiness and optimism actually fuel performance and achievement.

How do scientists define "happiness"? Scientists boil down happiness to the experience of positive emotions – *pleasure* combined with deeper feelings of *meaning* and *purpose*. Happiness implies a positive mood now and a positive outlook for the future. Franklin Roosevelt had the basic idea when he said "Happiness lies in the joy of achievement and the thrill of creative effort".

How Can we Increase Happiness and Create a More Positive Mindset?

Over 200 studies on over 275,000 people worldwide found that happiness leads to success in nearly every domain – including both profit and non-profit organizations! Research has found that our brains are hardwired to perform best when they are in a positive state, not negative or even neutral. How do we build more happiness into our lives and the lives of our team members? Here are some ideas that we can use ourselves and share with our team members (from Dr. Shawn Anchor's excellent book *The Happiness Advantage*):

Meditate/Pray: Research has shown that a few minutes per day of regular meditation can permanently rewire the brain to raise levels of happiness.

Find Something to Look Forward to: We know that often the most enjoyable part of any special activity is the anticipation. One study found that people who just thought about watching their favorite movie actually raised their endorphin levels by 27 percent. If you can't take the time out right nor for a vacation or a special night out with friends, put something on the calendar even if it's weeks out. Then whenever you need a boost of happiness, remind yourself about it (I know this works – I just thought ahead to my summer vacation with my family and I feel instantly happier!).

Commit Conscious Acts of Kindness: Research has shown that acts of *intentional* altruism (kindness) decreases stress and strongly contributes to enhanced mental health. You can try this for yourself by picking one day where you intentionally complete five acts of kindness. You may be surprised at your increased level of happiness – and the recipients of your kindness will feel happier too!

Infuse Positivity Into Your Surroundings: Our physical environment can have a significant impact on our mindset and sense of well-being. We can intentionally infuse our work areas with images that spark positive emotions – pictures of family and friends and pets, and reminders of our favorite sports teams or special experiences in our lives. Making time to go outside on a nice day is also uplifting. One study found that spending 20 minutes outside in good weather not only boosted positive mood, but also broadened thinking and improved memory. We can also change our surroundings to minimize negative emotions. A good place to start is to watch less TV. Studies have shown that the less TV we watch (especially violent and negative programs), the happier we are.

Exercise and Physical Activity: Exercise releases pleasure-inducing chemicals called endorphins and has other benefits. Physical activity can boost mood, improve motivation and feelings of mastery, reduce stress and anxiety, and help us get into a flow of engagement and productivity. One landmark study on depressed people showed that exercise was just as effective as anti-depressants in the short-run, and in the long-run exercise was significantly more effective.

Spend money (but not on stuff): Research has shown that money spent on activities (e.g. group dinners, concerts, sporting events) brought far more pleasure than material purchases like shoes, TVs or expensive watches. Spending money on other people also boosts happiness. This lines up with the biblical teaching that it's more blessed to give than to receive.

Exercise Signature Strength: Studies have shown that the more we use our signature strengths the happier we become. We all have multiple things that we are good at. Each time we use a skill we are good at we experience a burst of positivity. If you need a happiness booster, try using a talent you have not used for awhile.

Researchers have found that exercising strength of character is even more fulfilling than using a skill. A team of psychologists identified 24 character strengths that most contribute to human flourishing. They developed a 240 question survey that identifies a person's top five "signature strengths" (you can take this survey for free at www. viasurvey.org). In a study, volunteers were asked to pick one of their signature strengths and use it in a new way each day for a week. These volunteers became significantly happier and less depressed than controls groups. And these heightened levels of happiness remained six months later when re-examined.

Motivating Your Team

The best managers use the Happiness Advantage as a means to motivate their teams and maximize individual and team potential. Research has shown that even small moments of positivity in the workplace can enhance efficiency, creativity, motivation and productivity. One way to do this simply is to provide frequent recognition and encouragement. One study found that teams with encouraging managers performed 31 percent better than teams with managers who were less positive and less open with praise! Recognition can take many forms—verbal thanks, complimentary e-mails, written notes—and can include meaningful tokens of appreciation like gift cards, certificates of appreciation, or food.

Let me close with this perspective from Eleanor Roosevelt: "Since you get more joy out of giving joy to others, you should put a good deal of thought into the happiness that you are able to give." One of the great privileges we have as managers is to help bring increased happiness into the lives of our team members. It will benefit them individually and spark the team to new levels of performance.

Good luck to you as you use the fuel of happiness to drive yourself and your team to higher levels of success!

20

Are You Treating Your Employees Like Adults or Children?

"The best executive is the one who has the sense enough to pick good men (and women) to do what he wants, and self-restraint enough to keep from meddling while they do it."
—President Theodore Roosevelt

A while back I stumbled across a book entitled *30 Reasons Employees Hate Their Managers,* by Bruce L. Katcher. This book summarized the results of a large survey project across 65 organizations. The survey found that the biggest area of complaint employees have is feeling they are being treated like children, not adults.

I resonated with these survey results and remember back early in my career when I had my first opportunity to be a Supervisor at the tender age of 23. There was a lady on the team who had put in her resignation to work in another company just prior to my selection. I had heard about the value of doing exit interviews with departing employees, so I took her aside and asked her one simple question. "Why are you leaving?" Her reply was short and to the point. "I am leaving because I feel like I have been treated as a *child*, and I am going to a company that will treat me like an *adult*." I was speechless, but her sentiment has stuck with me years later.

Survey Says

The employee survey zeroed in on some sentiments that people feel. Included are feelings like "We feel like slaves," "I hate being micro-managed," "I am afraid to speak up," "Nobody appreciates my hard work," and "There are different rules for different people." Here are some of the specific results: 46 percent of employees felt management treated them with disrespect. 40 percent said they didn't have the decision-making authority they needed, and 43 percent said their good work went unrecognized. 52 percent did not feel free to voice their opinions openly.

A recent Gallup survey found that only 31 percent of workers say that are actively engaged on the job. That means 69 percent are disengaged—51 percent passively disengaged and 18 percent actively disengaged. Sad results. *I suggest that a big driver for this lack of engagement and low motivation is a result of being treated like children*. I think motivational expert Bob Nelson is right when he says, "An employee's motivation is a direct result of the sum of interactions with his or her manager."

Why do Managers treat employees like children and not adults? The reasons are many, including bad role modeling (how the Managers have been treated, and what they have seen), fear of delegation, lack of trust towards employees, and others.

12 Keys to help us Treat Employees like Adults

So how can we do a better job of treating employees like adults and not children? Let me share 12 keys to help us:

1) **Practice the Golden Rule.** Treating others positively like we would like to be treated is an ethical approach that crosses most religious and ethical frameworks. Consciously put yourself in the shoes of your employees and ask yourself: How would I like to be treated if I was in their jobs?

2) **Get to know your employees as people**. We are all very busy and no let up is in sight. But employees feel dignified and appreciated when we make an effort to get to know them as people—not just a worker producing widgets. This is a challenge for many of us, but practicing MBWA (management by walking around) and looking for opportunities to connect will help. I have also found it useful to do 1-on-1's with all my employees, both direct reports and "skip levels" with frontline employees.

3) **Treat employees like assets, not liabilities, and view them as valued business partners.** Some managers view their employees as liabilities—expenses that need to be minimized. Others view employees like assets that are worth being developed and maximized, which is a more dignifying view. Also, the managers that view their employees as valued business partners are naturally going to treat them more respectfully.

4) **Survey your employees.** Want to know how employees are really feeling? Ask them. Anonymous surveys can be great tools. We use quarterly employee satisfaction surveys, and annually we do a survey instrument like Gallup's 12 Question Measuring Stick. It's helpful as a Manager to periodically do

a 360 degree personal survey, with one group of respondents being your employees.

5) **Provide more opportunities for employees to have control.** Reality is that for some of our departments, especially in production type environments, we need to have some structure and rules to get the work done timely and accurately. However, employees do appreciate having as much control as possible over work schedules (including opportunity for part-time), time off, work space, overtime (voluntary versus mandatory), dress code, etc. *We should look for opportunities to grant employees some choices and control whenever we can.*

6) **Promote flexibility rather than rigid rules**. Rules do have their place and are needed to ensure some level of consistency and order within the organization. But sometimes we can be too rigid and too arcane, resulting in employees feeling like they are being treated like children.

I recently had a manager from Nordstrom in one of my University classes. Here are the rules he shared that are found in their employee handbook:

Rule #1: Use best judgment in all situations. There will be no additional rules. Please feel free to ask your department manager, store manager or division general manager any questions at any time.

Obviously we will need more rules than the Nordstrom example, but I think you get the point of trying to avoid too many rules and too much rigidity.

7) **Appreciate that employees have lives outside of work.** Our employees have lives outside of their vocational work with us, and they appreciate when we recognize that reality and work with them when "life happens". We appreciate the flexibility to attend to our life events, and so do our employees.

8) **Respect employee privacy.** All of us have expectations of the right to privacy. When there are good business reasons for some type of employee monitoring, we should be open about it. We should also not treat employees as our possessions and assume we can infringe on their privacy whenever we want.

9) **Be a Good Listener.** Ernest Hemingway advises, "When people talk, listen completely. Most people never listen." I like the practical advice from Dale Carnegie (author of the classic *How to Win Friends and Influence People*) who said, "You can make more friends in two weeks by becoming a good listener than you can in two years trying to get other people interested in you."

10) **Increase recognition and appreciation.** According to prominent psychologist William James the number one psychological need the average person has is the need to feel appreciated. A Gallup survey found that 65 percent of employees said they did not receive any positive personal recognition from their boss the prior twelve months. How sad! There are many ways to recognize employees, and some of the simple ones are the most appreciated. Verbal thanks, e-mails, and small tokens of recognition are always in order. And in today's digital age, the value of a hand written note or card has never been higher.

11) **Be honest with employees.** Research by Kouzes and Posner in their acclaimed book *The Leadership Challenge* shows

that people desire leaders who are honest, trustworthy and men and women of integrity. There is no place for lying to our employees. Sometimes we need to withhold information for a period of time (e.g. a re-organization that is still being worked on), but we should disclose information as soon as possible).

12) **Support professional development.** If we truly view employees as assets and valued business partners, it makes sense to support our employees in their professional development. There are lots of ways we can help develop employees, as I have written about in the past. Employees do feel valued when we are willing to provide them learning and development opportunities and show that we care.

Treating employees like adults, not children, is a great example of the "win-win" that Stephen Covey always emphasized. Employees that are treated like adults will have better morale, stronger motivation, higher productivity and more loyalty to the organization. Our teams will be stronger and our personal sense of accomplishment will be higher. I wish you success in striving for the worthy ideal of treating our employees like adults!

21

Treating Your Employees Like Valued Family Members

"Every single employee is someone's son or someone's
daughter. Like a parent, a leader of a company (or team)
is responsible for their precious lives."
—Simon Sinek, author of *Leaders Eat Last:*
Why Some Teams Pull Together and Other's Don't

In the previous lesson I dealt with the importance of treating our employees like adults, not children. I want to go beyond that and talk about the importance of *treating our employees like valued sons and daughters (i.e. family members)*.

I was inspired to explore this concept after interacting with my good friend Mark Fallon, who is the CEO of The Berkshire Company (Berkshire-Company.com), and reading the book he recommended called *Leaders Eat Last*.

Mark and I had the privilege of being featured speakers at a NACUMS annual conference (nacums.org). In one of my presentations I discussed the concept of treating employees like adults, and in one of Mark's he discussed the idea of treating employees like valued sons and daughters. In discussions afterwards we realized these two concepts go hand-in-hand. Let me share the importance and value of treating employees like valued family members (sons and daughters)—the "why"—and then share some ideas on the "how".

Why Is It Important to Treat Employees Like Valued Family Members?

When employees are not treated like trusted and valued members of a family, a number of negative consequences follow. The Deloitte Shift Index found that 80 percent of people are dissatisfied with their jobs. A recent Gallup poll showed only 31 percent are actively engaged on the job. There is an obvious correlation between job satisfaction and job engagement.

In addition, the landmark Whitehall studies showed that job stress was largely driven by the degree of control workers feel they have throughout their day. In a nutshell: less control, more stress. More job stress leads to higher levels of physical and mental illness. And studies show that a child's sense of well-being is affected primarily not by the hours that their parents put in at work but the moods they are in when they arrive at home. *By not adequately caring for our employees we are harming them—and their children!*

In contrast, the organizations that do treat their employees like valued family members develop a culture of empathy and mutual trust. A sense of family is developed where employees feel like they belong and feel valued and cared for. This caring environment allows people to fully engage their heads *and* their hearts. The good news is that there are organizations that set good examples for us in treating employees like valued family members: Costco, Southwest

Airlines, Nordstroms, Bob's Red Mill, Barry-Wehmiller and many others. Treating employees like valued family members leads to higher levels of employee engagement. What is the impact on the organization's performance? Gallup research showed that work units in the top quartile in employee engagement outperformed the bottom quartile units by: [1]

10 percent in Customer Ratings

22 percent in Profitability

21 percent in Productivity

25 percent lower turnover

37 percent less absenteeism

48 percent fewer safety incidents

41 percent less quality defects

How Do We Treat Employees Like Valued Family Members?

Following are eight guidelines that can help us treat our employees like valued family members (by the way—these are also great parenting tips for raising our kids!).

1) Avoid dehumanization – treat people like people. The employees that work on our teams are *people*, not numbers on a spreadsheet or machines that make widgets! As people they are created body, soul and spirit and have many roles, relationships and responsibilities—some involving their occupation and many more non-work related.

One of the most respected CEOs within the communication industry understood this concept well. Anne Mulcahy was the CEO who positively led Xerox from a place of weakness to a place of strength. Her following quote reveals a key to her successful philosophy: "Employees who believe that management is concerned about them as a whole person, not just an employee, are more productive, more satisfied, more fulfilled. Satisfied employees mean satisfied customers, which leads to profitability."

2) Treat with respect. Every person that works on our teams craves to be treated with respect and deserves respect. I resonate with Albert Einstein when he said, "Everyone should be respected as an individual," and also when he said, "I speak to everyone the same, whether he is the garbage man or the President of the University." One of the most practical ways to show respect to our employees is to *listen*, as this Bryant McGill quote emphasizes: "One of the most sincere forms of respect is actually listening to what another has to say."

Listening to and respecting our employees leads to people naturally working together to help each other and to advance the organization. Working with a sense of obligation is replaced with working with a sense of pride and teamwork.

3) Provide protection. One of the roles of parents is to help protect our children from the dangers lurking inside and outside the home. Likewise, a caring leader will do what she can to protect her employees from the dangers lurking in the work place, such as unnecessary micro-management, unreasonable job requirements, or negative work conditions. A caring leader will also try and provide protection from external dangers, such as overreaction to adverse economic conditions or unfair outsourcing attempts.

4) Clarify expectations and provide guidance. People need to know what the rules are and what results are expected. We all need clarity on expectations, and feedback when we are on course and when we are heading in the wrong direction.

5) Balance Care and Accountability. Just like we care for our real life family members, we should show caring towards our employees. Demonstrating consistent caring will help develop the family environment we should crave. At the same time, just as we hold our real life family members accountable for following our rules, values and goals, we need to do the same with our employees. When the caring is present, the accountability will be well received and help us maximize performance.

6) Reinforce and Reward Positive Behaviors and Results. Research has led to the development of what some have called the Greatest Management Principle in the World — *You get what you reward*. Sincere, regular and positive recognition, and rewarding of desired behaviors, is common sense — but not common practice. A Gallup poll of thousands of employees found that 65% claimed to have received no praise or recognition the past year!

7) Be Flexible and Willing to Adjust Your Style. I have two daughters. They have the same parents and grew up in the same home, yet that have a significant number of personality, behavior and style differences. Our employees also have differences, and we should try and communicate and connect in ways that best suit their individual differences and preferences.

8) Focus on "Positive Leading" over "Controlling Managing". Bob Chapman, CEO of Barry-Wehmiller, led the company in a remarkably positive turnaround. His main strategy was to treat employees like valued family members and develop a culture of empathy, caring and trust. The following quote of his really reso-nates with most people: "No one wakes up in the morning to go to work with the hope that someone will *manage* us. We wake up with the hope that someone will *lead* us!"

Treating employees like valued family members benefits them and us as leaders. Employees that are treated like valued family members will have better morale, stronger motivation, higher productivity and more loyalty to the organization. Our teams will be stronger and our personal sense of accomplishment will be higher. I wish you success in striving for the worthy ideal of treating your employees like valued family members!

22

Are You a Fred?
The Importance of Exceptional
Customer Service!

"There is only one boss – the customer. If we don't take care of our customers, someone else will."
—Sam Walton

Fred Shea was a postal carrier who really took to heart and embodied the following quote from Martin Luther King: "If a man is called to be a street sweeper, he should sweep streets even as Michelangelo painted or Beethoven composed music or Shakespeare wrote poetry. He should sweep streets so well that all the hosts of heaven and earth will pause to say 'Here lived a great sweeper who did his job well.'"

Fred provided exceptional service to all his customers, and constantly went the extra mile. He would even drive through the neighborhood to check on people on his days off! One of Fred's very satisfied customers was motivational speaker and author Mark Sanborn, who wrote a book about exceptional customer service called *The Fred Factor*. I highly recommend getting the book and video training series and going through them with your team.

Here are four cardinal principles about being a "Fred":

1) **Principle #1: Everyone Makes a Difference.** Every individual can choose to do his or her job in an extraordinary way, regardless of the circumstances.

2) **Principle #2: Success is Built on Relationships.** The quality of the relationship determines the quality of the product or service.

3) **Principle #3: You Must Continually Create Value for Others, and It Doesn't Have to Cost a Penny.** You can creatively find no-cost ways to exceed expectations of your customers.

4) **Principle #4: You Can Reinvent Yourself Regularly.** Every morning you wake up with a clean slate. We can choose to follow the advice of John Wooden's father Joshua, who taught, "Make each day your masterpiece."

One tool to measure how well your team provides customer service is to conduct a periodic customer survey. By analyzing the results of the survey, you can reinforce what is going well and identify areas that can be improved. Because people are busy these days, I prefer to keep the survey simple and short. Here is a sample survey that you can use as a starting place.

CUSTOMER SURVEY

Timeliness:
Are your jobs completed in a timely manner?

Below Expectations _____

Meets Expectations _____

Exceeds Expectations _____

Quality:

How is the overall quality of the work that our team provides for you? (same Below, Meets or Exceeds Expectations scale)

Responsiveness:

Is the staff responsive to your special requests? (same Below, Meets or Exceeds Expectations scale)

Helpfulness:

Do you find that our staff are helpful and offer solutions to your needs? (same Below, Meets or Exceeds Expectations scale)

Overall Performance: (same Below, Meets or Exceeds Expectations scale)

Are there services that you would like to see that are not currently provided?

What do you feel are some areas of strength in how we serve you?

What ideas do you have on how we can serve you better in the future?

Unfortunately Fred-like service is not common. As Roger Staubach says, "There are no traffic jams along the extra mile." Being a Fred is a choice. How will you and your team choose?

Let me close with a final quote to think about from Andrew Carnegie: "There are two types of people who never achieve very much in their lifetimes. One is the person who won't do what he is told to do, and the other is the person who does no more than what he or she is told to do". Good luck as you commit yourself and your team to go the extra mile and be "Freds"!

23

Want to improve Performance? Measure It!

"What gets measured gets improved."

—Peter Drucker

Peter Drucker was the considered the Father of professional management. He said "Leadership is lifting a person's vision to higher sights, the raising of a person's performance to a higher standard, the building of a personality beyond its normal limitations." Being in a management role provides us the opportunity to intentionally raise the performance levels of our teams and the individuals that comprise them.

To improve the performance of our teams, we need relevant performance measures to inspire, provide a common focus and allow us to track progress. Here are some tools to help develop powerful performance measures:

Ask the Right Performance Questions

Organizational Development expert Brad Fishel has developed the "Right Question" approach for optimal performance management. The Right Questions express the critical few things by which to judge our performance results. Put yourselves in the shoes of your key stakeholders (investors, customers, employees) and ask what is important to them?

When you answer the Right Performance Questions, realize that some measures you develop in response will be Quantitative (numeric) in nature (e.g. how many pieces of mail were produced last month), but some will be Qualitative (subjective) in nature (e.g. how useful are our reports?). Don't ignore qualitative measures; consider using word descriptions as metrics too. Brad says, "Better to have subjective judgments about important questions than objective data about unimportant questions."

Develop "balanced" measures to judge success.

Effective teams add value to all important stakeholders and avoid a singular focus (e.g. being low cost) to the detriment of other important outcomes (e.g. high quality). Following are potential types of measures to consider. For each measure that gets used, we should have a target (goal) to compare actual results against:

1) **Productivity** (productivity is simply a measure of Goods & Services produced, divided by Resources Used)

2) **Quality** (e.g. reliability, accuracy, mistake free, meets requirements, etc.)

3) **Volume** (how much is being produced)

4) **Timeliness** (work products completed when needed)

5) **Service** (customers satisfied with the service they receive)

6) **Compliance** (postal regulations, Sarbanes-Oxley, HIPPA, and other regulations being met)

7) **Cost** (e.g. measure overall costs and/or cost per unit)

8) **Safety** (e.g. lost work days; OSHA recordables)

Intentionally focus on improving performance.

How can we strive to improve productivity and overall performance? Following are some tools to choose from:

1) Lay out a challenge (illustrated by the closing story)
2) Enhanced Training & Development
3) Provide recognition and use incentives
4) Pursue wise use of technology
5) Look for process improvements
6) Be a better servant leader and show more care for your employees
7) Solicit ideas from your team members
8) Learn from other successful teams

Let me close with the following story from the life of Charles Schwab, former head of U.S. Steel. [1] Schwab said:

I had a mill manager who was finely educated, thoroughly capable, and master of every detail of the business. But he seemed unable to inspire his men to do their best. One day I asked him: "How is it that a man as able as you, cannot make this mill turn out what it should?" "I don't know" he replied. "I have coaxed the men; I have pushed them; I have sworn at them. I have done everything in my power. Yet they will not produce."

It was near the end of the day; in a few minutes the night force would come on duty. I turned to a workman who was standing beside one of the red-mouthed furnaces and asked him for a piece of chalk. "How many heats has your shift made today?" I queried. "Six" he replied. I chalked a big "6" on the floor, and then passed along without another word. When the night shift came in they saw the "6" and asked about it. "The big boss was in here today", said the day men. "He asked us how many heats we had made, and we told him six. He chalked it down."

The next morning I passed through the same mill. I saw that the "6" had been rubbed out and a big "7" written instead. The night shift had announced itself. That night I went back. The "7" had been erased, and a "10" swaggered in its place. The day force recognized no superiors. Thus a fine competition was started, and it went on until this mill, formerly the poorest producer, was turning out more than any other mill in the company.

24

Want to Increase the Productivity of Your Team? The Key is You!

"The productivity of work is not the responsibility of the worker, but of the manager."
—Peter Drucker

Continually increasing productivity is always important—even more so in tough economic times we often live in. The good news is that by being intentional almost every team has the potential to increase their productivity. Paul J. Meyer was right when he said, "Productivity is never an accident. It is always the result of a commitment to excellence, intelligent planning, and focused effort." Before sharing ideas on how to improve productivity, let's first define it.

Productivity Defined

Productivity is a measure of how efficiently resources are being used. Productivity is simply a measure of Outputs (goods/services produced) divided by Inputs (resources used):

P = O (goods/services) / I (resources)

For example:

Assume that last month it took 10,000 labor hours to produce 500,000 mail pieces. What is the productivity measurement?

$P = \underline{500,000}$ mail pieces = <u>50 mail pieces per labor hour</u>
10,000 labor hours

How to Improve Productivity

There are two basic approaches to improving a productivity measurement. One, increase the volume of goods/services without increasing the amount of resources used. The second approach is to produce the same volume of good/services, but accomplish with fewer resources.

One way to try to improve productivity is to conduct a "factor analysis", i.e. look at the following seven factors and identify areas for improvement. For example, perhaps the better utilization of Technology could increase productivity. The solution may be to provide training to employees that will help them better understand how to use technology to increase their productivity.

Some of the factors that have a bearing on productivity include:

1) **Technology.** The wise use of automation and more sophisticated software can help us complete our work with fewer labor hours. Just this month I have been able to reduce (redeploy to another department) an FTE on one of my teams due to new software that is more efficient than the existing software.

2) **Capital (tools, equipment, etc.).** Having state-of-the-art equipment that fits your operations can open the door to significant reductions in manual effort and resources.

3) **Methods.** Learning and applying best practices, and pursuing process improvements can drive improved efficiency and productivity. You can learn better methods by attending conferences like MAILCOM and National Postal Forum, getting involved with professional organizations like Mail Systems Management Association and Postal Customer Councils, and regularly reading trade journals.

4) **Quality.** Improving the quality of work outputs can lead to better productivity. Why? It's cheaper and more efficient to do the work correctly the first time and avoid re-work. John Wooden's quote, "Be quick, but don't hurry," is applicable. Also, by instilling a quality mind set I have found the teams take more pride in their work and become more engaged and productive.

5) **Management.** Being a better servant leader and showing more care for your team members will pay dividends. Collaboratively developing a shared vision and challenging yet achievable goals will help inspire your team to higher levels of performance. Solicit ideas for improved productivity from your team members. They will feel respected, and you will glean some great ideas along the way.

6) **Motivation of workers.** Providing positive recognition and showing more care for your employees will lead to a higher morale, higher motivation—and higher productivity. I agree with Tom Peters, who said, "The simple act of paying positive attention to people has a great deal to do with productivity." Remember to measure productivity and celebrate improvements along the way. Celebrating progress builds a sense of achievement and a desire to keep getting better.

7) **Skills/expertise of team members**. The on-going training and development of your team members is key to enhancing productivity. I have addressed this in detail in other chapters. A few ideas include the usage of some team meetings for training, cross training, participating in trade associations, sending people to conferences and relevant seminars, university courses, mentoring—the list goes on.

Let me share a final tip to improve the productivity of your team. Paul Gauguin wisely said "Stressing output is the key to productivity, while looking to increase activity can result in just the opposite." Focusing on effectively and efficiently producing output, while minimizing resources used, will result in increased productivity.

Good luck as you partner with your team and intentionally pursue a higher level of productivity and performance!

25

Justifying Resources: An Ongoing But Winnable Battle

"If you don't go after what you want, you'll never have it.
If you don't ask, the answer is always no. If you don't
step forward, you're always in the same place."
—Nora Roberts

Managing operations can be very rewarding as well as very challenging. In my conversations with managers across the country, one challenge constantly surfaces: justifying the resources (people, budgets, and equipment) needed to run an excellent operation. This is one of the biggest challenges that I face too, but there are some ways to be successful in acquiring the resources you need.

Before we dive into the specific tips, here are two general principles: First, normally we will not get anything if we don't ask. Second, we need to make sure that, when we do ask, we are asking for resources that benefit one or more of key our stakeholders: **investors**, **customers**, **employees** and the **community** we do business in. Here are some tips that can help you improve the probability of acquiring the resources that you need to benefit stakeholders.

Ten Tips to Justify What You Need

1. **Identify the important goals, initiatives, values and business needs of your organization, then figure out how to help meet them**. What are the major goals, initiatives and values of your organization? Can you find ways to help your organization be more successful? Linking the resources you need to specific corporate goals and initiatives will help build a compelling business case for authorizing funds.

    For example, many organizations have some form of customer focus or engagement initiative. I have recently justified new equipment and enhanced software in part so that our company can provide more personalized and relevant communication with our customers. Many organizations have a strong emphasis on sustainability. Finding ways to use physical mail prudently and avoiding waste will be positively received. In the past, I have received approval for a second printer so we could go from two-page simplex bills to one-page duplex bills.

2. **Find ways to save your organization money**. An almost sure-fire way to justify a proposed expenditure is to demonstrate that it will result in savings to your organization. Portland General used to pay external vendors 50 to 60 cents per color copy. My team developed a proposal to lease color digital printers and showed that we could provide color copies at a significant savings. We have also found ways to save money

by offering CD burning services, scanning services, and by maximizing postal discounts. If you are not maximizing the pre-sort and automation postal discounts, investing in relevant software and/or sorting equipment can often be economically justified due to the incremental postage savings.

3. **Know your costs and how they compare to the external marketplace.** This is huge. If you can demonstrate that your internal operations are less costly than the potential external providers are, then you have the ammunition to justify the funds to keep your operations performing well.

4. **Work with vendors for creative ideas to improve your operation and document justification.** Vendors can be a great resource of ideas and can be very helpful in developing justification for proposals. Vendors like Xerox, Pitney Bowes and Ricoh have helped us develop creative ways to improve the quality and efficiency of our operations in cost-effective ways. Developing positive relationships with your current vendors and other potential new vendors can pay huge dividends. One of the benefits of going to conferences like MAILCOM and National Postal Forum is the opportunity to meet vendors and pick up ideas and build relationships.

5. **Partner with other departments within your organization.** Sometimes other departments may have special needs for printing, mailing or fulfillment. These needs should be viewed as potential partnering opportunities.

We experienced a "win-win" opportunity awhile back. The Mapping department needed a new large document printer to print large maps and was planning to purchase a printer and then hire a person to run the printer. My printing department had a really old large document printer that needed replacing. So, we offered to house the new printer at our shop and run for no cost to that department. They accepted the offer, and we gained a new printer that benefits the entire company.

You should also look for other partners and advocates within your organization—Marketing, Customer Service and Relations, Public Relations, Corporate Communications, etc. Enlisting the support of these internal advocates shows decision makers that your requests have broad support.

6. **Develop positive relationships with internal "service providers" that influence decisions**. Most organizations have a financial staff that plays an important role in the approval process of budgets and capital requests. Human Resources usually gets involved with decisions to upgrade and/or add staff. Legal, Purchasing, Corporate Communications and other staff areas also play key roles. These service providers can be your allies or foes–the choice is largely up to you.

   You can improve your relationships with these individuals by practicing the 3 "Rs" of recognizing, respecting and rewarding. Individuals from these functions often have degrees and/or certifications and feel a sense of professional pride. Recognizing them as experts and professionals by seeking their counsel and appreciating their expertise will pay dividends. Treating them positively and respectfully will enhance relationships. And when someone does help you, showing your appreciation in a tangible way (e.g. verbal thanks, email, card, gift certificate, or food) does wonders for the relationship.

7. **Take the budgeting process and other "bean counting" tasks seriously**. Many operational managers detest budgeting, accounting and those "bean counting" tasks. But a sure-fire way to develop better credibility with your finance staff is to learn how to develop accurate budgets and be able to explain budget variances and provide future forecasts.

   How can you improve your ability to budget? By carefully reading the documentation that is provided, asking questions, involving other people in the process (staff, management chain, vendors) and by documenting your assumptions. The pay-off is worth the extra effort–if you improve your credibility with the finance folks, they will be more likely to become advocates of your requests, not adversaries.

8. **Understand your organization's budgeting and approval system and processes.** Become well versed on the criteria used for making decisions, and the necessary format and content of required documentation. Know who the key decision makers are, and genuinely seek to build positive relationships. Following the time frames and playing by the rules will help build your credibility and improve your odds at getting needed approvals.

9. **Track your volumes and document increases.** Sometimes decision makers operate under mistaken assumptions, such that hard copy mail and printed pages are disappearing and no longer important. The facts can speak for themselves, so track the volumes of all the work you do and use as part of your overall business case to justify your requests.

10. **Build a good business case!** Complete a stakeholder analysis and explain the benefits and Return-On-Investment (ROI)

as relevant to investors, customers, employees and the community. Be sure to include both *quantitative* (financial) and *qualitative* (non-financial) benefits. Reference the advocates that support your requests.

One bonus tip: intentionally work to build the credibility of you – and your team. Refer to lesson #38 *"Credibility – Our Passport to Respect and Achievement"* for ideas to increase your credibility. Establishing credibility with the decision makers is extremely important and will increase your success rate. Justifying resources is never easy, but consistent application of these ten tips will help. Good luck in your journey to develop a quality operation that adds value to your stakeholders!

26

Change Management: A Key to a Successful Future

"If you don't like change, you will like irrelevance even less."
—General Eric Shineski

One of the most challenging yet important roles for us in management is to effectively lead necessary changes. Change management is not easy—but it's very important and there are tools we can use to be successful.

What is change management? Wikipedia defines it as, "approach to transition individuals, teams and organizations to a desired future state." Let's explore this topic by looking at why change management is important, then we'll explore some tools to help us excel.

Why Change?

We need to change in order to be successful in a future that is different than what we have experienced in the past. President John F. Kennedy drove that point home when he said, "Change is the law of life, and those who only look to the past or present are certain to miss the future."

We also need change to continue to improve our teams and better meet the needs of our stakeholders. Often change is not appealing, but it's needed to move ahead. Charles Kettering explained, "The world hates change, yet is the only thing that has brought progress." Let's look at some models and tools to help us successfully lead and manage change.

John Kotter's Eight Step Change Model

Dr. John Kotter is a Harvard Business School professor and leading thinker and author on organizational change management. Kotter's eight-step change model is highly regarded and considered by many to be the definitive change model. His model includes the following eight steps:

1. **Create sense of urgency**. Help explain why change is necessary. Includes the problem of the status quo and the desirability of a better future. President Ronald Reagan once quipped. "Status quo, you know, is Latin for 'the mess we're in.'"

2. **Build the guiding team.** Find effective change leaders. Get the right people in place with the right emotional commitment, and the right mix of skills.

3. **Create a vision for change.** Really explain the "why" for the change, and then develop an understandable vision and strategy to achieve the vision.

4. **Communicate the vision.** Communicate the vision frequently and powerfully. Address people's concerns and anxieties openly and honestly.

5. **Remove obstacles.** Take action to quickly remove barriers. Recognize and reward those who are making change happen, and identify resisters and help them see what's needed for success.

6. **Create short-term wins**. Nothing motivates more than successes so celebrate positive achievements. One of my key principles is that "success breeds success".

7. **Keep change going.** Embrace and promote the philosophy of continuous improvement. Set goals to build on the momentum you've achieved.

8. **Make change stick.** Reinforce the value of the successful change, and make sure relevant policies, procedures and practices are being followed.

ADKAR Change Model

Prosci's ADKAR model is a coaching tool to help guide employees through the change process. ADKAR has ability to identify why changes are not working and help you take the necessary steps to make changes successful. ADKAR stands for:

A = Awareness of need to change

D = Desire to participate and support the change

K = Knowledge of how to make the change

A = Ability to implement the change

R = Reinforcement to sustain the change

The ADKAR components are progressive. In other words, the first step in the change process is Awareness for the need for change, then Desire to participate and support the change, etc. You can periodically survey your employees and evaluate how they are coming along in the change process. For change to be successful, we need to help lead all of our team members along each of the change steps.

Leadership Role in Implementing Change

Multiple studies have concluded that the number one key to a successful change initiative is effective leadership and management sponsorship. Leaders need to communicate, advocate and ensure overall awareness of the change process. I think Socrates was on target when he said, "The secret of change is to focus all your energy, not on fighting the old, but building the new."

Following are important roles for leaders to fill well:

Communicator: Communicate with change leaders, project team and key stakeholders. Explain why the changes are needed and risks of not changing. Correct misinformation as it arises.

Advocate: Demonstrate support for the change through words and actions.

Liaison: Balance the needs of both project and business teams to achieve goals.

Coach: Coach employees through the change process. Includes coaching people to prepare for changes in their roles and explaining new performance expectations.

Resistance Manager: Identify and manage resistance. Respond to questions and concerns.

Personal Change Management Example

About three years ago I had a change in management responsibility and inherited some teams that needed to make some changes. Recent benchmarking had confirmed that the teams were very *effective* and did quality work. But benchmarking also confirmed that the teams were not as *efficient* as some of our peers.

The starting place for affecting change is to make the case for change. In this case, we emphasized the need to become more efficient based on what was best for our key stakeholders. Customers would benefit by paying less for the services we provide. Shareholders would benefit from lower costs. Employees would benefit from being part of industry leading teams that would not be future targets to be outsourced (i.e. higher job security). To become more efficient we needed to reduce staff, and have reduced 20 percent of our staffing all through attrition—no involuntary lay-offs! To accomplish this, we have clarified expectations, increased performance monitoring and coaching, and provided extra doses of positive reinforcement. Some members of the teams were at or nearing retirement and decided it was a good time to retire, which ended up being a win-win for them and the teams. Intentionally working through the ADKAR process, and being intentional about having supportive change management, have been keys to a successful change. I am especially gratified by two facts: 1) Our performance metrics have not suffered, in fact in some cases have improved, and 2) A recent Job Satisfaction survey showed that overall job satisfaction was actually slightly higher than it was before the change effort! Much of the credit rests with the team Supervisors who have done excellent work, showing high levels of care and accountability.

Managing change is not easy, but if done well pays huge dividends for all involved. Good luck as you pursue changes that add value to your team and its stakeholders!

27

Checklists - Simple Tools with Complex Benefits

"Everywhere I looked, the evidence seemed to point to the same conclusion. There seemed to be no field or profession where checklists will not help."
—Atul Gawande, author of the bestseller
The Checklist Manifesto: How to Get Things Right

Looking for a simple tool that will drive your operations to higher levels of efficiency and effectiveness? The checklist may be what you are looking for. Awhile back I read Atul Gawande's *The Checklist Manifesto* and was inspired to read real-life examples from the medical field, construction, aviation, finance and others to show how simple checklists—coupled with timely and effective teamwork—can vastly improve the quality and effectiveness of what we do, and in some cases, literally make the difference between life or death.

Atul, a surgeon, shared how he and his team developed a two-minute checklist that covered some basics for surgery (*e.g.*, do we have enough blood and antibiotics?), as well as some basics for good teamwork (*e.g.*, does everyone in the Operating Room know the name of each person in the room?). They then tested these lists in eight different hospitals. The results were stunning. When they took the time to make introductions and follow the checklist, they had a 35 percent *decline* in deaths and complications related to surgery!

The Problem: Avoidable Mistakes

The problem is that mistakes are being made that harm people and our organizations. Why? In part because we are trying to do more with the same or less resources. Also, the pace of life has increased with the always evolving know-how and sophistication. People's expectations are rising, and so has our struggle to deliver on them.

You see it in the mistakes authorities make when hurricanes or tornadoes or other disasters hit. You see it in the increase in lawsuits against attorneys for legal mistakes—the most common being simple administrative errors, like missed calendar dates and clerical screw ups, as well as errors in applying the law. You see it in flawed software design, in our struggling financial institutions—in fact, in almost any endeavor requiring complexity and significant amounts of knowledge.

The communication world, including print, mail and e-communications, has not been exempt from errors. We have recently seen a large company mistakenly mail out thousands of mail pieces with sensitive customer information; but unfortunately, information was sent to the wrong customers and a security breach transpired. Sad to say, this example within the communication industry is not an isolated one.

Avoidable mistakes are common and persistent, not to mention demoralizing and frustrating to employees and customers alike. And the reason for mistakes seems to be clear—the volume and complexity of what we know has often exceeded our individual ability to deliver its benefits correctly, safely, or reliably. Knowledge has both helped us and burdened us. We need a tool to help us navigate complexity and avoid unnecessary and harmful mistakes.

The Solution: Checklists

Checklists by themselves are not the proverbial "silver bullet" that will eliminate all mistakes, but they will help reduce mistakes and improve our quality and effectiveness. I have had multiple teams earn Quality certifications like the MPTQM (Mail Processing Total Quality Management) from the Postal Service and ISO-9001. A key component to earning these certifications and ensuring consistent quality in our operations is the use of checklists. Our ultimate goal is not just to have people ticking boxes on a checklist. *Our ultimate goal is to have our teams embrace a culture of teamwork, discipline and quality*, and checklists can be a useful means to that end.

Benefits of Checklists

One of the benefits of checklists is that we can help prevent mistakes *before* they occur, versus cleaning up mistakes after the fact. My philosophy simply stated is, "The more time and effort we spend on *proactive fire prevention*, the less time and energy we need to spend on *reactive firefighting*."

Here are some of the specific benefits of checklists. Checklists:

1) Help with memory recall and clearly set out the necessary steps in a process. This provides verification and helps ensure consistency.

2) Establish standards of good performance and help ensure proper execution.

3) Help defend everyone, even the experienced, against making mistakes. Help combat complacency.

4) Serve as a "cognitive net". They catch mental flaws inherent in all of us—flaws of memory, attention and thoroughness.

5) Serve as a great training tool to help ensure people are completing tasks correctly.

For me *the bottom line is that checklists can help eliminate "stupid" mistakes*. In some fields like medical, aviation and construction, these avoidable mistakes have not only cost organizations millions of dollars—they have also cost people their lives. In our industry, normally lives are not at stake, but service to our customers, avoiding risk, making money for our shareholders, and creating a high performance culture for our employees is on the line.

Checklist for Developing Checklists

A key to successful checklist development is *participation,* especially with the end users of the checklist. Participation builds buy-in and support and will result in better quality end results.

You can go to gawande.com, download Atul Gawande's "A Checklist for Checklists", and also see a few sample checklists. Let me share some key questions (guidelines) in building effective checklists:

Step One: Development

- Do you have clear, concise objectives for your checklist?
- Is each item a critical step and in danger of being missed? Not adequately checked by other mechanisms? Actionable, with a specific response needed?

- Have you involved all relevant team members in the checklist creation process?

Step Two: Drafting

- Does the Checklist utilize natural breaks in workflow (pause points)? Use simple sentence structure and basic language? Have a simple, uncluttered, and logical format? Fit on one page? Minimize the use of color?
- Is the font sans serif, upper and lower case text, large enough to be read easily and dark on a light background?
- Is the date of creation (or revision) clearly marked?

Step Three: Validation

- Have you: tested the checklist with front line users (either in a real or simulated situation)? Modified the checklist in response to repeated trials?
- Does the checklist fit the flow of work? Detect errors at a time when they can still be corrected?
- Can the checklist be completed in a reasonably brief period of time?
- Have you made plans for future review and revision of the checklist?

Checklists aren't the total solution to eliminating mistakes. But they are an important tool to helping us and our team members from making those "stupid" mistakes that are easy to make when we're working hard and trying to keep up with the many details of getting the work done. Good luck to you as you expand the use of checklists and lead your team to an even higher level of quality and performance!

28

Delegation: A Win-Win Management Tool!

"Delegation is the most powerful tool leaders have."
—Dr. John C. Maxwell, Leadership author and speaker

Want to maximize your personal productivity and develop your team members at the same time? Delegation is a key management tool to use. Delegation doesn't come naturally to many of us. We often think it's safer and easier to do things ourselves. Eli Broad observes, "The inability to delegate is one of the biggest problems I see with managers at all levels."

Trying to do too much and not delegating is not a recent problem—it dates back at least 4,000 years to the days of Moses. In Exodus chapter 18 we read the story of Moses leading the nation of Israel and trying to do it all, to the detriment of the people. Moses' father-in-law Jethro came to visit and saw the dysfunction. Jethro recommended that Moses delegate some of the responsibilities and authority to other capable men and reserve the really big issues for himself. Moses wisely listened to the advice of Jethro, and the Israelites were the benefactors.

Let's explore the management tool of delegation by asking and answering some fundamental questions: *Why* delegate? *When* to delegate? *What* to delegate? *Who* to delegate? And *How* to delegate?

Why Delegate?

Delegation done well benefits you and the person you delegate to. A big benefit for leaders is it frees us up to do the value-added tasks we are paid to do. It helps us avoid being spread too thin and burning ourselves out. Anthea Turner was on the mark when she said, "The first rule of management is delegation. Don't try and do everything yourself because you can't." We also gain the satisfaction of seeing team members grow and develop.   Perhaps the main benefit to the person we delegate to is they get the opportunity to grow and develop as they learn and apply new skills, gain additional experience, and enjoy the fruits of their labor. Successful completion of delegated tasks builds confidence and improves morale and motivation.

When to Delegate?

When should we look to delegate? Here are some questions to consider that may help you decide when to delegate:

1) Is someone else capable to do the job or is it a job that only I can do?
2) Is there someone else that can do the job better than me?
3) Is there someone else who can do the job at a lower cost than me?
4) Is there someone who could benefit from the opportunity to learn and grow by doing this job?

5) Do I have enough time to delegate the job effectively? This would include adequate time for training, questions and answers, and opportunities to check progress.

What to Delegate?

The reality is there are some tasks that we should NOT delegate even if we could. Tasks that are very important to the success of your team should not be delegated (participation by others yes, delegation no). Tasks like strategic planning and selection of team members should be led by the team leader and not delegated.

We should avoid delegating menial or unpleasant work just because we would prefer not to do it. On the other hand, delegating work that is value added, reasonably challenging, and rewarding can provide a person an opportunity to feel trusted and to learn and grow.

Who to Delegate?

Delegation to the right person can be inspiring and provide an opportunity to help their development and prove themselves worthy of greater future responsibilities—and a task gets completed competently. Delegation to the wrong person can result in poorly completed tasks and frustration by you and them. To help find that right person consider some of these factors:

- Does a person have the experience, knowledge and skills to competently perform the task?
- What are the person's goals and aspirations? Would this delegation be helpful to them in meeting their goals and aspirations?
- What is the current work load of the person? Do they have time to meet the expectations of the task?

How to Delegate?

There are key components to delegation that will help ensure success. Following are some of the most important steps to successful delegation:

- **Understand the job to be delegated.** We need to be clear in our mind what needs to be done, the process to follow and who we want to do the work.

- **Clearly explain the assignment and explain the "why".** We should meet with the employee and explain why this is an important assignment, then talk through expectations on the desired end result. Don't forget to review the process. This includes levels of delegated authority (e.g., what decisions can be made by the employee versus decisions requiring Manager approval), progress updates, your availability for support, etc.

- **Confirm understanding and commitment.** We should make sure the assignment and all expectations are understood—and the employee is committed to see the assignment through to successful completion.

- **Monitor progress and provide on-going feedback.** We want to ensure that the assignment gets completed in accordance with expectations. We also want the employee to learn and have a positive and confidence-building experience. Providing on-going coaching will help this be the "win-win" we are looking for. We also want to avoid what I call "dirty delegation"—micro-management and not letting go enough of the task. The other extreme to avoid is "reverse delegation" which occurs when the employee entices the manager to do the task that was intended to be delegated.

- **Evaluate performance and identify lessons learned.** Once the assignment is completed it is valuable to collaboratively discuss performance of the employee and discuss lessons learned. The time to reflect, evaluate and discuss outcomes and lessons learned is where much of the value of delegation lies.

- **Don't forget to say "thanks!"** Last but not least, don't forget to say "thank you" to the employee! People crave appreciation and recognition, and providing that will be motivating and inspiring to the recipient.

Here is a final inspiring quote from John Maxwell: "If you want to do a few small things right, do them yourself. If you want to do great things and make a big impact, learn to delegate." I wish the best for you and your team as you delegate well!

29

Conflict: A Potential Blessing in Disguise

" ... We can work it out. Life is very short, and there's
no time for fussing and fighting my friends."
—John Lennon & Paul McCartney

Conflict is an inevitable part of human relationships and exists in every organization and team. The good news is conflict handled well can be healthy and lead to greater successes. Bad news is that conflict handled poorly can result in employee dissatisfaction, lower productivity, poor customer service, increased employee absenteeism and turnover, increased stress and in worst case litigation based on claims of harassment or hostile work environment.

Let's start with a discussion of when conflict can be healthy. Healthy conflict occurs when there is a work environment where people can voice disagreements and have candid conversations about the important issues at hand. A healthy exchange of ideas and different viewpoints can result in sharper analysis, more creativity and well-crafted initiatives moving forward.

Steve Goodier speaks to the value of different perspectives: "We don't get harmony when everybody sings the same note. Only notes that are different can harmonize. The same is true with people." The key is to disagree without being disagreeable, and once decisions are made to have everybody support them.

Since there is potential for conflict to bring benefits when handled well, let's look at some keys to resolving conflict.

Keys to Resolving Conflict Well

Here are some guidelines to resolving conflicts and gaining some benefits when they arise.

1) **View Conflict as an Opportunity.** Leadership guru Warren Bennis cuts to the chase, saying, "Leaders do not avoid, repress, or deny conflict, but rather see it as an opportunity." Healthy conflict resolution can improve the quality of our processes, initiatives and relationships—and make our teams stronger.

2) **Pick Your Battles.** Some conflicts are minor and will resolve themselves without our intervention. Sometimes the best action we can take is no action.

3) **Hit Conflict Head On.** If a conflict is important enough to be addressed, don't avoid it but take it on and drive to a peaceful resolution. Unresolved conflicts can escalate and become harder to resolve as time drags on, so we are wise to resolve sooner versus later.

4) **Stay Calm.** Conflicts escalate when we get angry. And we tend to stop listening to understand as we get angry. To remain calm it's helpful to look at the big picture and realize

that most disputes eventually get resolved and very few have long-lasting consequences.

5) **Listen to Understand.** One of Stephen Covey's 7 Rules of Highly Effective people is to "Seek first to understand, then to be understood". Dean Rusk counseled, "One of the best ways to persuade others is with your ears—by listening to them." By active listening we dignify people and give them a chance to fully share their perspectives. We also build the foundation that can lead to acceptable resolutions.

6) **Ask Good Questions and Gather Information.** Few conflict situations are clear cut, so we need to ask good questions and gather information before jumping to conclusions. Good questions focus on asking what happened and soliciting relevant information. Open-ended questions such as, "Can you tell me what happened?" can draw out useful information in a non-judgmental manner.

7) **Attack the Problem, not the Person.** Personal attacks backfire, as Abigail Van Buren emphasized when she said, "people who fight fire with fire usually end up with ashes." Remember the goal is to resolve the conflict and underlying problems, not to punish the people who are involved in the conflict.

8) **Identify Points of Agreement and Disagreement.** Henry Ford observed, "If there is any secret of success, it lies in the ability to get the other person's point of view and see things from that person's angle as well as your own".

9) **Look for the Win-Win.** Edwards Deming encouraged us to "Adopt a new philosophy of cooperation (win-win) in which everybody wins." Greg Anderson explains. "The Law of Win/

Win says, "Let's not do it your way or my way; let's do it the best way."

10) **Be Creative.** Try brainstorming and thinking outside the box to find creative resolutions. Being creative with resolutions takes longer, but can yield a true win-win solution.

11) **Focus on the Future, not the Past.** The secret to conflict resolution is to treat it like problem solving and focus on what can be done to resolve the immediate problem at hand. Once that is done, look at the past to analyze what went wrong, and then identify improvements so that future results meet expectations.

12) **Celebrate Agreement.** Reaching mutual agreement on what we will do to resolve the conflict is often stressful and hard work! Reaching agreement is also valuable and worth taking the time to celebrate—which may be as simple as a hand shake, fist bump or high five.

13) **Develop a Resolution Plan.** Once we have mutually agreed upon the resolution to the conflict, we need to document a resolution *plan* so there are clear action steps and assignment of responsibilities. Having a plan will increase the probability of the resolution being implemented as agreed upon.

14) **Execute the Plan and Follow-Through.** Plans by themselves have little or no value unless they are executed. This is an extremely important step, where we sometimes fall short. We need to diligently "*plan the work, **then** work the plan*" as my former boss and mentor Bruce Carpenter emphasized.

15) **Reflect and Derive Lessons Learned.** After the resolution plan is executed and the dust settles there is great value in taking time to reflect and identify lessons learned. Much of

the value that comes from conflicts is the after-the-fact reflec-
tion and identification of lessons learned that can help us be
better managers and improve the success of our teams in
the future.

Most of us don't like when conflict happens, but when it does let's
look for the hidden blessings and use it as an opportunity to make
ourselves and our teams stronger for the future!

30

Managing Operations in Tough Economic Times

"Tough times never last, but tough people do."
—Robert H. Schuller

The recent recession has impacted us all. Our companies, our teams and our personal lives all felt the hit (remember watching your 401-k shrink before your eyes?). During tough economic times, seems like everybody is focusing on holding the line or cutting costs, and the media bombards us with negative news on a constant basis.

How can we be more effective managers when the tough times hit? Here are some tools and techniques that may prove useful.

1. **Communicate, Communicate, Communicate**. Studies have shown that employees want to know how the team and the organization are doing, and the person they most trust for this information is their immediate supervisor. Our employees want to hear both the positive and negative news from us. If we fail to communicate, a vacuum is created, and that vacuum

is filled by the "rumor mill", which invariably is negative and destructive to morale and motivation.

2. **Give Your People Hope**. Napoleon said, "Great leaders are dealers in hope." We don't want to sugarcoat current realities, but we can share the strategies in motion to make the future brighter. We can also remind people that every prior recession has been followed by several years of growth and prosperity.

3. **Dole out hugs and practice random acts of kindness.** I ran across this quote from Robert Thompson, professor of Popular Culture from Syracuse University: "Whenever there is a big national moment of crisis, whether it's a terrorist attack or a global recession, what flows is a period of consciousness-raising. This whole situation has put the entire country in a state where everybody desperately feels the need for a hug."

    As leaders we can generously give out verbal, written and even physical "hugs" to our team members. What the great philosopher Plato said years ago is especially relevant today. "Be kind, for everyone you meet is fighting a hard battle." Putting our emotional intelligence to work will help build camaraderie and ease a bit of the pain that people are feeling.

4. **Manage Your Costs.** Everybody is feeling the pressure to hold the line on costs, or even lower costs. One key to manage costs is to invite your employees into the process. It's surprising the good ideas that employees come up with if you are candid with them and invite their participation. For example, my company needed to cut our Operating Budget by $25 million during the peak of the recession. We shared

the need with employees, brainstormed, and came up with the budget cuts without any employee layoffs.

Here are a few cost saving ideas my teams implemented at the time: reduction of overtime by process improvements and awareness of need to cut back; reduced employee business expenses by scaling back purchased food and outside meals. In some cases food was eliminated, in other cases employees have brought in food items on their own dime. We also saved on training and development costs by focusing on the most value-added uses of our training dollars, such as local events and resources. One team eliminated a recently vacated position. The team came up with process improvements and unanimously agreed to fill in the gap.

Another challenge is the replacement of capital equipment. One key is to ensure you have a strong preventative maintenance program in place, which may extend the life of equipment until capital funds become available. When you are ready to make a request for capital funds, build a good business case including how your costs compare to an outside vendor. Doing a multi-year Net Present Value (NPV) comparison is helpful, assuming your NPV of costs is lower than what an external vendor would charge.

5. **Consider Insourcing or Outsourcing.** Insourcing involves bringing in work from another company. If you have a well-managed operation and have available capacity, bringing in external work can leverage your assets and provide a means to subsidize your costs.

   Another alternative to consider is outsourcing. Ask the following questions: Do we have a high quality and low cost in-plant operation? Is our company committed to the in-plant operation and keeping up with best practices and industry trends? Is our company willing to invest in vintage replacement of equipment? If your answer is "yes" to all these questions, then keeping the in-plant is likely the best option. But if you have any "no" answers, outsourcing the operation to a vendor or another in-plant may be the best choice.

6. **Build up morale, motivation and productivity through Recognition.** Other lessons deal with the topic of recognition in some detail. Here are a couple of key points: Research over the years has led to the development of what some have called the "Greatest Management Principle in the World". *You get what you reward.* Sincere, regular and positive recognition and rewarding of desired behaviors is common sense, but not common practice. A Gallup poll of thousands of employees found that 65 percent claimed to have received no praise or recognition the past year!

On-going recognition and praise makes a person feel appreciated and important, and stimulates the intrinsic motivation to excel. Gallup research found that individuals who receive regular recognition and praise:

- Increase their individual productivity
- Increase engagement among their colleagues
- Are more likely to stay with their organization
- Receive higher loyalty and satisfaction scores from customers
- Have better safety records and fewer accidents on the job

Tough economic times eventually come to an end. Meanwhile, we have the opportunity to make a positive difference within our organization and help navigate through the tough waters we are sometimes in. Let me close with a favorite quote from Vince Lombardi: "When the going gets tough, the tough get going." Economic tough times are for managers to get going!

31

The Management Wisdom of Benjamin Franklin

"An investment in knowledge always pays the best interest."
—Benjamin Franklin

A couple of years ago I had the privilege to speak at and attend the MAILCOM conference (mailcom-conference.com), which I do frequently. One of the presentations by industry expert Marlene O'Hare focused on how the practical wisdom of Benjamin Franklin can help us manage our operations well. With her blessing I want to share some of Franklin's advice which I have found to be useful and inspiring.

Benjamin Franklin was not only a Founding Father of our country—he was also the first Postmaster General of the United States, as well as a very successful businessman, leader, inventor, writer and person. He is considered one of the smartest and wisest men our country has ever produced!

We can learn a lot from Franklin that can help us be better managers and help our operations be even more successful. Following is a list of some tips inspired by his wisdom.

Benjamin Franklin's Keys to Management and Operational Success

Strive for Excellence. "Whatever you become, be good at it." Excellence does not happen by chance. We must intentionally choose to excel at what we do, including making the choice to become more effective leaders and managers.

Be Prepared. "By failing to prepare, you prepare to fail." A plan is needed to accomplish our goals. Charging in without any thought to the end result and how to achieve it is a sure way to fall flat on your face.

Don't Fight Change. "When you are finished changing, you are finished." Change is inevitable. Focus on proactively making positive changes, and avoid being only reactive, thus having changes thrust upon you.

Less Talk, More Action, and Actions Speak Louder than Words. "Well done is better than well said." We all know that talk by itself is cheap. Talking about a project doesn't get it done. We must take action see the work through.

Don't Procrastinate. "Never leave till tomorrow what you can do today." It's easy to fall into the procrastination trap. One tip to avoid this trap is to have time-specific and measurable goals. And when you achieve key milestones or goals, remember to take time to reward yourself and enjoy the sense of achievement.

Be Organized. "For every minute spent in organizing, one hour is earned." "A place for everything, everything in its place." To maximize our productivity and achievement of our goals, we need to take the time to plan and to organize our resources. The time we spend planning and organizing our work really does come back to us with interest.

Avoid Busywork. "Never confuse motion with action." Our time is limited and the expectations on us keep growing. We need to use our time well by avoiding unnecessary tasks, delegating when it makes sense, and focusing our attention on the highest value work.

Give Yourself Permission to Make Mistakes. "Don't fear mistakes." "You will know failure. Continue to reach out." Fear of making mistakes can immobilize us. Taking risks and making mistakes provide us a special learning opportunity — provided we learn from the mistakes and grow from them.

Know Yourself. "There are three extremely hard things: steel, a diamond, and to know one's self." Self-awareness is the first tenant of emotional intelligence. Be honest with yourself, and seek input from others regarding your strengths and areas for further development.

Get Moving. "All mankind is divided into three classes: those that are immovable, those that are moveable, and those that move." Which class do you fall into? The most successful people in life are those that actually move and get things done.

Act Quickly on Opportunities. "To succeed, jump as quickly at opportunities as you do at conclusions." Opportunities are everywhere. Our challenge is to be quick enough and smart enough to seize them when they arise.

Engage Your Staff Actively. "Tell me and I forget; teach me and I remember; involve me and I learn." Experiential learning is at the core of developing ourselves and our team members. Give people a chance to learn by doing real work. Reinforce what they did well and patiently coach them when they could do better.

Don't Give Up. "If at first you don't succeed, try again." "Energy and persistence conquer all things." Striving to achieve our goals can be downright exhausting, right? There are times when we all feel like throwing in the towel. But pushing through those down times will eventually result in significant achievements. When we look back, we will say it was worth the effort.

Wise Up. "Life's tragedy is that we get old too soon and wise too late" and "I wish I knew then what I know now." We can accelerate our acquisition of wisdom by intentionally seeking out growing experiences, and by taking time to reflect on what we have learned from our experiences. We can also tap into the wisdom of others who have gone before us by reading their words, listening to them speak into our lives, and observing their actions.

Be Smart. "The only thing more expensive than education is ignorance." Franklin modeled being a life-long learner. We can take advantage of traditional education sources like colleges and universities, plus we can attend relevant conferences. We can also read trade journals and good books. It's not enough to hear a good idea—the real value comes when we put it into practice.

Keep Trying. "Diligence is the mother of good luck." One tip is to break down our bigger goals into small units of work and then complete them one at a time. Another tip is to choose to forego some of our time spent in front of the TV, PC or I-Pad and concentrate on getting our priority goals completed.

Seek Knowledge and Wisdom. "If a man empties his purse into his head, no one can take it from him." "The doors of wisdom are never shut." We have many potential sources to learn and develop more wisdom. Take advantage of them! In addition to our personal life experiences, we can *learn from the experiences of others* through mentoring, involvement in professional associations, attending conferences, taking classes and workshops, and reading what they write about their experiences and lessons learned.

The final piece of advice I wanted to highlight is the encouragement to continue to grow as a person. Franklin said, "Be at war with your vices, at peace with your neighbors, and let every new year find you a better man." Good luck as you continue on your journey to be a better manager—and person!

PART THREE:

PERSONAL FOUNDATION LESSONS

"Never try to be better than others, but be the best you can be."
                                        —John Wooden

"We are either progressing or retrograding all the while; there is no such thing as remaining stationary in this life."
                                        —James Freeman Clarke

"Practice the philosophy of continuous improvement. Get a little bit better every single day."—Brian Tracy

32

Understanding Ourselves and Others

"He who knows others is wise.
He who knows himself is enlightened."
—Lao Tzu

Having a high level of Emotional Intelligence (EQ) is essential to being an effective Manager, and EQ starts with having accurate self-awareness. Self-awareness can help us gain self-control and be helpful to people around us—not hurtful.

Some tools to help expand our self-awareness include: get feedback from others, such as using 360 degree surveys; have a mentor to speak into your life; and constantly seek feedback from others on how we are doing. The Apostle Paul articulated a worthy goal: "Do not think of yourself more highly than you ought, but rather think of yourself with proper judgment."

Another tool to better understand ourselves is to take one or more of the Personality type tests, such as Meier-Briggs or Perspectives. The most credible test according to researchers and experts in the field is the "Big Five Personality Trait" model. Taking this test and analyzing the results will help increase your self-awareness. I suggest discussing your results with some people with whom you work closely, and listen to their feedback—both positive reinforcement and constructive suggestions. Then intentionally work at leveraging your potential strengths and mitigating your potential weaknesses.

Big Five Personality Trait Model

You can take the Big Five Personality Trait test and get your results for free at the following web site: outofservice.com/big five. Here is an overview of the five dimensions and their meanings.

Agreeableness. This dimension refers to an individual's tendency to get along well with others. Highly agreeable people are likable, cooperative, warm and trusting. People who score low on this dimension tend to be cold, disagreeable and antagonistic.

Extraversion. This dimension captures our comfort level with relationships. Extraverts tend to be outgoing, social, friendly, affectionate and assertive. Introverts tend to be reserved, non-assertive and quiet.

Emotional Stability. This dimension taps a person's ability to withstand stress. People with positive emotional stability tend to be calm, self-confident, optimistic and secure. Those with high negative scores tend to be nervous, anxious, dissatisfied and insecure.

Openness to Experience. This dimension addresses the tendency to be original, have broad interests, be daring and take risks. Extremely open people are creative, innovative, curious and artistically aware. Those at the other end of this scale are more conventional and find comfort with the familiar.

Conscientiousness. This dimension is a measure of reliability. A highly conscientious person is responsible, organized, dependable and persistent. Those who score low are easily distracted, disorganized and unreliable.

Big Five Traits and Work Performance

Research on the Big Five model has found correlations with these personality dimensions and job performance. The Big Five trait most consistently related to work performance is conscientiousness. This trait is as important for managers as it is for front-line employees. The most effective performers score high in this dimension in the form of persistence, attention to details and setting of high standards. Highly conscientious people learn more and develop higher levels of work knowledge, which contributes to higher levels of job performance.

Other findings show that people who score highly on emotional stability are happier than those who score low. Emotional stability is the trait most strongly related to life satisfaction, job satisfaction and low stress levels. Extraverts tend to be happier in their jobs and in their lives overall, and tend to emerge more often as leaders than as introverts. People scoring highly on openness to experience are more likely to be effective leaders. Agreeable people are happier and better liked than disagreeable people.

The experts say that if we are intentional, we can modify our natural tendencies and become more effective. For example, I naturally tend to score lower on Openness to Experience. I have intentionally pursued new experiences to help gain the benefits and become more balanced on this dimension.

Use Big Five Test to Help Others

In addition to using the test for yourself, why not use it with your key team members? Helping them better understand themselves is valuable for their own self development. It also can help you better synchronize strengths, weaknesses and tendencies and develop a more powerful team.

I have used this model with my leadership team. I explained the model, and then had them take the test and do their own self-analysis. We then shared our individual results and provided feedback and shared suggestions. It's a great tool to help the members better understand and support each other.

Let me close with a quote from tennis star Billie Jean King: "I think self-awareness is probably the most important thing towards being a champion (or a great manager!—my addition)." Good luck on your journey of increasing your self-awareness and effectiveness!

33

Keys to Developing Good Relationships

"Treasure your relationships, not your possessions."
—Anthony J. D'Angelo

People are naturally social creatures. We crave friendship and positive interactions, just as we do food and water. The better relationships we have in life, including in the workplace, the happier and more successful we will be. President Teddy Roosevelt was on the mark when he said, "The most important ingredient in the formula of success is knowing how to get along with people."

How can we build stronger relationships that will help us be more successful and add value to the people we are trying to serve in our lives? Let me share Twelve Principles of developing good relationships that may be helpful.

Twelve Principles to Build Good Relationships

Here are twelve principles that can help build good relationship with people:

1) **Develop Your People Skills.** Good relationships start with good people skills. People skills are primarily "soft skills" like collaboration, communication and conflict resolution. How do we assess our current level of people skills and identify areas for improvement? Having trusted mentors or close friends that have the freedom to speak into your life is helpful, as is periodically taking confidential surveys and soliciting honest feedback.

2) **Develop Relationships with All People.** Some people are very status conscious when it comes to building relationships. These people focus on establishing relationships with people perceived to be important in the hierarchy, while those viewed as low on the totem pole are given little attention. But the people we most admire are those who treat *all* people as important. I resonate with Bill McCartney, who said, "Anytime you devalue people, you question God's creation of them." And I agree with Ann Landers: "The true measure of a man is how he treats someone who can do him absolutely no good."

3) **Be a Giver, not Merely a Getter.** Commit to being a *servant leader*, giving of yourself to help meet the needs of others. We can give of our time, knowledge and resources to help people around us. Giving of ourselves is the ultimate win-win that benefits both the receiver and the giver. Winston Churchill said, "We make a living by what we get. We make a life by what we give." Anne Frank reminded us that, "No one has ever become poor by giving." And A.L. Williams encourages us that selfless giving also benefits us when he said, "The greater you help others, the greater your own success."

4) **Employ Active Listening Techniques.** Carefully listening to what people are saying is crucial to developing good relationships. Rachel Naomi Remen emphasizes the importance of listening when she advises, "The most basic and powerful way to connect to another person is to listen. Just listen. Perhaps the most important thing we ever give each other is our attention ... A loving silence often has far more power to heal and to connect than the most well-intentioned words." Active listening techniques include maintaining good eye contact, asking clarifying questions, and repeating back to the person what you think you heard him or her say.

5) **Promote Open and Effective Communication.** The starting place in developing open and effective communication is to be a good listener as we just covered. In addition, relationships are enhanced when we encourage people to freely express their thoughts in a non-judgmental manner. It's also important to communicate with respect, and to stay rational and avoid being overly emotional.

   Also, we all have our preferred channels of communication (e.g. face-to-face, phone, e-mail, texts, etc.), so using preferred channels can enhance communication effectiveness.

6) **Work on Building Trust.** Trust is foundational to good relationships. Tips to build trust include: consistently follow through on what we say we will do; never break confidences; and avoid bad-mouthing others behind their backs.

7) **Get to Know People on a Personal Level.** To really develop good relationships with others, we need to find ways to get to know people on a personal level (within reasonable boundaries). Asking non-probing, open-ended questions is a good

starting place. Then look to build bridges and find connections. Joseph Newton said, "People are lonely (disconnected) because they build walls instead of bridges".

To build bridges that connect you to people in a lasting way, share common experiences with them. Share meals. Go to a ball game or other events together. Take people to meetings with you. Participate on work projects together. Anything you experience together helps create a common history and builds connections.

8) **Be Mindful – and Know When to Dial It Back.** Being mindful means taking responsibility for our words and actions. Those who are mindful are careful and attend to what they say, and they don't let their own negative emotions impact the people around them. Being mindful also includes knowing when to have fun and when to be serious, when to be over the top and when to be invisible, and when to take charge and when to follow.

9) **Appreciate Others.** Showing sincere appreciation whenever someone helps you opens the door to great relationships. Prominent psychologist William James spent much of his career researching what our deepest needs were, and landed on the need for appreciation being at the top of the list for most of us.

10) **Be Positive, not Negative.** Focus on being positive. Positivity is attractive and contagious, and it will help strengthen relationships with those around you. On the other hand, no one wants to be around someone who's negative most of the time.

11) **Be Willing to Compromise.** Compromise involves each party getting something that he or she wants, so that everyone

wins (think Stephen Covey's "win-win" concept). People are drawn to those that are not self-centered and who are willing to put relationship over having everything done their way.

12) **Practice Common Courtesy.** A simple exchange of smiles and a "Hi" can be the first step in building a relationship. Making eye contact, saying "thank you" and picking up after yourself are also common courtesies that bring people together. Zig Ziglar was right when he said, "When you choose to be pleasant and positive in the way you treat others, you have chosen, in most cases, how you are going to be treated by others."

Building better relationships with people will enhance your influence and help you have greater success in achieving your goals. How will you use your greater influence? I resonate with Booker T. Washington, who said, "Those who are happiest are those who do the most for others." I wish you the best as you pursue better relationships with people and add even more value to the lives of people around you!

34

Are You Connecting?

"The best way to lead people into the future is to connect with them deeply in the present."
—James Kouzes and Barry Posner,
authors of *The Leadership Challenge*

H enry Kissinger said, "The task of the leader is to get his/her people from where they are to where they have not been." How can we help our co-workers be successful here in the present—and move with us towards a better future? A big key is for us as leaders to build strong *connections* with people.

How can we build strong connections and earn trust so that we can effectively influence our people to be successful? Let me share Ten Principles of connecting with people that I think can be helpful.

Ten Principles to Connect Well with People

1) **Commit to Connect.** The starting place for developing stronger connections with people is to make a conscious choice to do so. *Do you really want to connect better? If yes,*

commit to taking intentional steps to build deeper connections. The other principles will give you ideas to consider.

2) **Develop a Genuine Care for People.** We can only connect well with people when we value and care for them. We need to not take people for granted, but let them know we care and appreciate them. Valerie Elster reminds us that, "Expressing gratitude is a natural state of being and reminds us that we are all connected."

Maya Angelou wisely stated, "People will forget what you said, people will forget what you did, but people will never forget how you made them feel." Part of caring for people is to be honest, genuine and transparent. Let people see your heart of caring and compassion, and they will respond and feel closer to you. One of my often used quotes is that, "People don't care how much you know until they know how much you care."

3) **Be Proactive—Initiate Movement Towards Them.** It's tempting to sit back and let others try and connect with us. But as leaders we need to be proactive and take the initiative. Management experts Tom Peters and Nancy Austin concluded that, "The number one managerial productivity problem in America is, quite simply, managers are out of touch with their people and out of touch with customers."

4) **Look for Common Ground.** Probably my favorite leadership expert is John Maxwell. I agree with John when he says, "Anytime you want to connect with another person, start where both of you agree. And that means finding common ground." There are lots of potential areas of common ground,

ranging from personal interests to life experiences to values and beliefs. The key to finding common ground? *Listening.*

5) **Be a Good Listener.** Ralph Nichols advises that, "The most basic of all human needs is the need to understand and to be understood. The best way to understand people is to listen to them." When we listen to people they feel respected and we have a better connection with them. Bryant McGill makes that point when he said, "One of the most sincere forms of respect is actually listening to what another has to say."

6) **Recognize and Respect Differences.** While we should be looking to find common ground with others, we also need to acknowledge that we're all different. Our differences and diversity make our lives more interesting, and can strengthen our team performance as we blend our diverse backgrounds and abilities together to make us stronger.

7) **Share Common Experiences.** To really connect well with others, we need to find a way to cement the relationship. Isaac Newton cautioned, "We build too many walls and not enough bridges."

   A great way to build bridges with people is to share common experiences with them. Consider fun activities like bowling, playing Bunko, or going to a movie or sporting event. Work on special projects together. Celebrate together when a project gets completed or an important goal is reached. Common experiences build better connection and relationships.

8) **Get Out of Your Office.** Reality is that there are increasing expectations on managers to produce more results with the same or fewer resources. That can drive us into our offices to get our personal work done. But we need to intentionally

carve out times to practice **MBWA** (Management by Walking Around). I have to admit that I'm not as consistent in getting out of my office and touching base with people as I would like. How are you doing?

9) **Be a Giver: Provide Help and Share Knowledge and Resources.** Commit to being a *servant leader* who gives of oneself to help meet the needs of others. We can give of our time, knowledge and resources to help people around us. Giving of ourselves is the ultimate win-win that benefits both the receiver and the giver. Winston Churchill said, "We make a living by what we get. We make a life by what we give." Anne Frank reminds us that, "No one has ever become poor by giving."

10) **Once Connected, Move Forward.** There is value in building deeper connections with people just for relationship sake. But there is even more value when we use our connections with people to add value to our team's key stakeholders (investors, customers and employees) and drive towards a better future. Someone once said "Leadership is cultivating in people today a future willingness on their part to follow you into something new for the sake of something great." Connection helps create that willingness.

Building deeper connections with people will enhance your influence and help you have a greater impact. How will you use your greater impact? I resonate with Jackie Robinson when he said, "A life isn't significant except for its impact on other lives." I wish you the best as you pursue deeper connections with people and add even more value to the lives of people around you!

35

In Praise of Praise

"If managers want to create a workplace environment where people thrive, tap into the benefits of praise. It costs nothing and pays big dividends to both giver and receiver."
—Ken Blanchard, management consultant, speaker and writer.

Lee Iacocca once said, "Management is nothing more than motivating other people." Even though this statement is an over-simplification of what effective management entails, motivation is extremely important. So how do we create a work environment that people will find motivating? Some feel that finding fault and pointing out errors is the key to motivating. But focusing on the negative and downplaying the positive is not the answer. Johann Wolfgang Goethe emphasized the point when he said, "Correction does much, but encouragement does more."

Why Praise and Recognition Are Important

According to Tom Rath from Gallup, research has shown that, "Employees who report receiving recognition and praise within the last seven days show increased productivity, get higher scores from customers, and have better safety records. They're just more engaged at work."

Praise and recognition supports a "high-expectation, high-support" philosophy that can maximize long-term *results* **and** *relationships*. This approach *starts* with setting expectations and goals with employees – but doesn't *end* there. Setting a goal starts the behavior, but what happens next drives actual performance. Offering timely and specific praise as progress is made towards the goal will improve performance at every stage.

Another benefit of expressing praise and recognition is that every time we show people we care, it's like making a deposit in an emotional bank account. Making these deposits is important when you need to make a withdrawal by giving negative feedback. Gray Ridge, CEO of the WD-40 Company explains it well, "If you don't have enough emotional deposits, when you have that tough conversation, it's going to feel like an attack and it's going to hurt. But if you have enough deposits, the employee will already know that you mean them no harm and instead recognize that you're trying to help them."

Receiving praise and recognition benefits the *receiver* – but also benefits the *giver*. Recent research by the University of Pennsylvania on happiness and well-being found that the act of expressing gratitude is a major contributor to overall happiness. Researcher Sonja Lyubomirsky found that people who express gratitude are likely to be happier, more hopeful and energetic, and to feel positive emotions more often. They are also more forgiving, empathetic and helpful while being less depressed, envious and neurotic.

Keys to Effective Praise and Recognition

Effective praising should be sincere, specific, timely, frequent, based on current performance and personalized to the receiver.

Ken Blanchard, Vicki Stanford and David Witt have developed a TRUE Praise model which can help us be more effective in giving praise and recognition.

Timely: Praisings must be immediate and specific. Tell people exactly what they did right as soon as possible. For example, "You submitted your report on time Friday, and it was well-written. I was able to present your data at the meeting." Statements like, "Keep up the good work," are less sincere and not specific enough to be effective.

Responsive: Find out how people want to be praised. If someone doesn't like to be praised in front of peers, then the praising should be delivered privately. The point is to be aware of the needs of the people receiving the praise so it is meaningful to them.

Unconditional: Deliver praise without evaluation or strings attached. Praise should not be given with something expected in return. It should be given freely when deserved.

Enthusiastic: Give sincere and well-intentioned praise. Speak from the heart and tell people how you feel about what they did. For example, "I was so proud of you after hearing your financial report presentation. I want you know how good I feel about having you on our team."

The Five-to-One Ratio

Over the past decade, scientists have explored the impact of positive-to-negative interaction ratios in our work and personal life. They have found that this ratio can be used to predict—with remarkable accuracy—everything from workplace performance to divorce. And independent research has determined the ideal ratio for success and happiness to be **five** positive comments for every one negative (i.e. 5 to 1 ratio).

Researchers and consultants Emily Heaphy and Marcia Losada examined the effectiveness of 60 leadership teams. The driver that distinguished the most successful teams from the least successful teams was the ratio of positive comments to negative comments. Top performing teams gave each other more than five positive comments for every criticism, while the lowest performing teams gave each other three negative comments for every positive one.

Psychologists Donald O. Clifton and Tom Rath wrote the book *How Full is Your Bucket*. Included was their research into what the positive-to-negative ratio should be to maximize productivity and well-being. Guess what they concluded? Five-to-one ratio, positive over negative.

Researcher John Gottman has studied relationships for over 40 years, and has also found the magic ratio to be five positive for every negative. In one specific study using the 5:1 ratio, which Gottman dubbed "the magic ratio", he and his colleagues predicted whether 700 newlywed couples would stay together or divorce by scoring their positive and negative interactions in one 15-minute conversation between each husband and wife. Ten years later, the follow-up revealed that they had predicted divorce with 94 percent accuracy!

Why are so many positive comments needed for every negative one? People are emotionally conditioned to absorb the negative more deeply than the positive. If you reflect back on your own life experiences, you will know this is true.

Bringing it Home

The starting place to see more frequent praise and recognition in our work place is for us as leaders to set the example. Gandhi was right when he said, "You must be the change you wish to see in the world."

I would like to close with a couple of quotes from two of our country's most successful entrepreneurs and business leaders. Mary Kay Ash said, "There are two things people want more than sex and money ... recognition and praise." Sam Walton advised us to " ... appreciate everything your associates do for the business. Nothing else can substitute for a few well-chosen, well-timed, sincere words of praise. They're absolutely free and worth a fortune." I wish you well as you model and develop a culture of praise within your team!

36

Appreciating Appreciation

*"The deepest principle of human nature is a
craving to be appreciated."*
— William James, esteemed Psychologist

I t is a known fact that appreciation is one of the top motivators for
people to work harder and be more committed to their organizations. Studies show that appreciation is linked to happiness in the
workplace—and job satisfaction and engagement.

However, while 51 percent of managers feel they do a good job
of recognizing a job well done by their staff, only 17 percent of the
employees in the same groups believe their managers recognize them
for doing a good job.[1] Sadly, a Gallup survey found 65 percent of
respondents said they received NO appreciation from their boss the
prior 12 months! Let's dig into why appreciation is important and
look at principles to practice appreciation well.

Why Is Appreciation Important?

A study by career site Glassdoor revealed that more than 80 percent of employees are motivated to work harder when their boss shows appreciation for their work. The number one reason why employees enjoyed their work was, "I feel genuinely appreciated by the company."[2] On the other hand, 64 percent of employees who leave their jobs say they do so because they don't feel appreciated.[3] According to a study conducted by Towers Watson, the single highest driver of engagement is whether or not workers feel "their managers are genuinely interested in their wellbeing."

Ten Principles of Appreciation

Following are ten helpful principles of appreciation which are adapted from Barbara Glanz's book *The Simple Truths of Appreciation*.

1) **Everyone Wants and Needs Appreciation.** Steven Covey emphasized the need for appreciation when he said, "Next to physical survival, the greatest need of a human being is to be understood, to be affirmed, to be validated, to be *appreciated*."

2) **It Doesn't Have to Be Something Big**. Sometimes a simple compliment can be very encouraging. Mark Twain was quoted as saying, "I can go two months on one compliment." Samuel Taylor Coleridge inspired when he said, "The happiness of life is made up of minute fractions—the little soon forgotten charities of a smile, a kind look, a heartfelt compliment, and the countless infinitesimals of pleasurable and genial feeling."

3) **Make It Personal**. The best approach is to speak a person's appreciation language. See the section about the Five Appreciation languages.

4) **Be Creative**. Have fun at showing appreciation! You can organize fun outings, bring in food, give out certificates of appreciation—the list goes on.

5) **Surprise People if You Can**. One of the highlights of my career involved a surprise act of appreciation for a company Purchasing specialist (Frieda) who had been helping us with implementing RFPs in my Print & Mail Services department. The department Supervisor Eric and I invited Frieda to a meeting with us, where we proceeded to give her a dozen long-stemmed roses! She will never forget that—and neither will I.

6) **Be Sincere**. Sincere appreciation will be well accepted, but insincere appreciation can actually be worse than no appreciation at all. Bob Nelson encourages us to, "Take the time to appreciate employees and they will reciprocate in a thousand ways."

7) **Have a Plan.** One of the keys to doing appreciation well is to be consistent, and consistency requires intentionally planning ahead.

8) **Share Yourself—From the Heart.** Allow your emotions to show when expressing appreciation. When we show our hearts to our employees they are drawn to us and feel closer.

9) **Make It Memorable.** Look for opportunities to make a lasting memory. Thirteen years ago my Billing departments were working hard to try and implement a new Customer Information System. One afternoon to show my appreciation I took the teams out to see a movie, and sent them home early. I still hear positive feedback about that years later!

10) **You Will Receive More Than You Give.** Pat Boone was right on when he said, "The most attractive people in the world are those who are interested in others—turned outward in cheerfulness, kindness, appreciation, instead of turned inward to be constantly centered in themselves." Jesus taught that it is more blessed to give than to receive, and we know from experience that is true.

The Five Languages of Appreciation

Psychologists Gary Chapman and Paul White identified five ways to show appreciation at work in their book *The 5 Languages of Appreciation in the Workplace*. They found that each person has a primary and secondary language of appreciation. Our primary language communicates more deeply to us than the others. Although we will accept appreciation in all five languages, we will not feel truly encouraged unless the message is communicated through our primary language.

1) **Words of Affirmation**. Includes using words to communicate a positive message to another person. Can include praise for accomplishments ("Thank you for completing the report completely and ahead of schedule"), or affirmation of character ("I appreciate the way you patiently help out your co-workers"), or personality traits ("One of the things I admire about you is your optimism in the face of change").

2) **Quality Time.** Means giving a person your focused attention and spending more time, discussing the topics that are relevant and important to them.

3) **Acts of Service.** This language involves reaching out to help others—providing practical help and going out of our way to lend a hand.

4) **Tangible Gifts.** Giving the right gift to a person who appreciates tangible rewards can send a powerful message of thanks, appreciation and encouragement. The important thing is to give something that is meaningful and relevant to them.

5) **Appropriate Physical Touch.** Caution is in order, but some team members respond well to appropriate physical touch, like high-fives, fist bumps and pats on the back. We frequently see this in the sports world, but it also can translate to the work environment.

How can you discover what your co-workers' appreciation language is? You could buy copies of the 5 Languages of Appreciation book, which includes access to an online assessment survey. Alternatively, you could explain the 5 languages and ask employees what they think their primary and secondary appreciation languages are. You can also observe a person's behavior, observe what they request of others and listen to their complaints to get clues to their preferred language.

Here is a closing thought. Appreciation is a *gift* you can give to anyone you encounter. It's completely your choice. And each time you choose to thank someone for a job well done, you are making the world a better place. Voltaire stated it well when he said, "Appreciation is a wonderful thing: it makes what is excellent in others belong to us as well." Thank you for "appreciating appreciation" and putting it into practice!

37

Are You A Trustworthy Manager?

"To be trusted is a greater compliment than to be loved."
—George MacDonald

We face an ongoing challenge to building a trustworthy team that reliably serves our key stakeholders. The starting place to building a trustworthy team is to have it led by a trustworthy leader— you! How can we develop a higher level of trustworthiness for ourselves and our teams? Let me share some ideas, largely based on the work of Dr. Robert Hurley, a highly respected professor, consultant and former manager.

Six Keys to Building Trustworthiness

Here are the important six keys to build trustworthiness.

1) *Create Similarities: establish common values and a common identity.* Research has shown that we tend to trust people we think are similar to us and share our values. High-trust leaders and high-trust organizations create bonds of trust by developing and gaining commitment to common values and beliefs.

My company (Portland General) years ago established a core set of values which we call "Guiding Behaviors". These shared values have served us well over the years and saw us through challenging times such as the collapse of our one-time parent company, Enron. Here are PGE's "Guiding Behaviors":

- Be Accountable
- Dignify People
- Earn Trust
- Team Behavior
- Positive Attitude
- Make the Right Thing Happen

One value people desire, and which leads to being trusted, is honesty. Honesty is truly the best policy. Harvey S. Firestone drove the point home when he said, "I believe fundamental honesty is the keystone of business."Another tactic to build a common identity is to encourage people on your team to know each other as people, not just as professionals. Look for common experiences and interests that can help build a sense of camaraderie.

2) **Align Interests with those whose trust you want.** It is much easier to trust people that we feel will serve our interests. When interests are well aligned, it is much easier to trust. To build trust, start by clarifying and aligning stakeholder interests and promote those interests in a fair manner.

3) **Develop Benevolent Concern.** People tend to trust those who care about their welfare—those that demonstrate a benevolent character. If you want to earn trust, demonstrate that you will do the right things for others even if it puts you at risk.

Anthony J. D'Angelo was right on when he said, "Without a sense of caring there can be no sense of community." Jim Collins in his classic book *Good to Great* refers to the most effective leaders as "Level 5". Level 5 leaders are driven and at the same time humble. Their motivation is not self-gratification but building an organization bigger than themselves. Being devoted to others and to a larger mission at one's own expense breeds trust and loyalty.

4) **Develop and Demonstrate Capability to deliver on your promises.** We need to deliver on our commitments to develop trustworthiness. Want to earn trust? Prove that you can reliably deliver on promises, and don't make promises that you cannot keep. Remember the principle of "under promising and over delivering".

People are looking for leaders who know where they are going, and can instill confidence so that the team can be successful if they stay focused. To build confidence and trust a leader must:
- Think strategically about the future and anticipate change.
- Break changes down into manageable initiatives that can be implemented over time.
- Stay focused and execute.
- Mobilize groups of people in a change process.
- Develop and maintain good relationships.

An important element of maintaining trust is to be self-aware and humble. When leaders are comfortable enough to acknowledge areas where they are not competent, and then delegate and empower others to compensate, they build trust.

5) **Create a Track Record of Predictability and Integrity.** To earn trust, our actions must have a predictable pattern. An important part of predictability is integrity—honoring your word. High-trust managers always try to honor their word, and if they fail to do so they apologize and make sure it does not become a habit. Integrity also includes always doing the right thing, even if it costs you personally. As respected Senator Alan K. Simpson said, "If you have integrity, nothing else matters. If you don't have integrity, nothing else matters."

6) **Communicate – and do it clearly and openly.** I appreciate the advice I received from Portland General's highly respected CEO Peggy Fowler several years ago. She said there were three keys to being a great leader and manager: 1) communication, 2) communication and 3) guess what? Communication.

As a general principle it is better to *over* communicate versus to *under* communicate. If we fail to communicate adequately the gap is filled by the grapevine (i.e. rumor mill), and the rumor mill is invariably negative and demoralizing. Here are Dr. Hurley's five keys to being a trustworthy communicator:
- Share information
- Tell the truth
- Admit mistakes
- Give and receive constructive feedback
- Maintain confidentiality

Our teams will better serve our stakeholders if operating in a culture of trustworthiness. The key to developing a culture of trust is for us as leaders to be trustworthy ourselves. The road to being trustworthy is not always an easy one, but it's the right one for us to be on. Good luck to you as you pursue building greater trustworthiness in your team and in you as the leader!

38

Credibility: Our Passport to Respect and Achievement

"Credibility is the foundation of leadership."
—Kouzes and Posner, authors of *The Leadership Challenge*

Webster's dictionary defines credibility as "the quality or power of inspiring belief." Developing our credibility is a necessary ingredient to earn respect and pave the way for greater achievement for ourselves and our teams. Greater credibility leads to greater influence and management effectiveness, and aids our efforts to justify resources and find support for our initiatives.

Credibility is built upon two twin pillars: 1) character and 2) competence. Both character and competence are important, and go together like peanut butter and jelly, or Laurel and Hardy (imagine one of those without the other!).

Following are ten building blocks that will help develop our character and competence, and build credibility in the process.

215

Ten Building Blocks for Developing Credibility

1) **"Walk the Talk".** Multiple surveys have shown that people are looking for leaders with integrity and trustworthiness—those that live out strong personal ethics and always strive to do the right things. Alan Simpson says, "If you have integrity, nothing else matters. If you don't have integrity, nothing else matters!" How true!

2) **"Be a Straight Shooter".** The Bible speaks of "speaking the truth in love." Being candid AND dignifying leads people to trust what we say. Always telling the truth is important—one lie can sink us. Wes Fessler says, "Credibility is like glass. It is strong until it is broken, and then it is almost impossible to repair."

3) **"Beat the Grapevine".** It is better to over communicate than to under communicate. When we fail to communicate thoroughly a vacuum is created, and that hole gets filled with the grapevine (rumor mill) which is invariably negative and often wrong.

4) **"Mess up? Fess up!"** We are all human and make mistakes. Credible people don't lie or hide from their blunders. Brian Koslow says it well: "The more you are willing to accept responsibility for your actions, the more credibility you will have."

5) **"No Excuses—Make It Happen".** Michael Jordan said, "Some people want it to happen, some wish it would happen, others make it happen." Credible people are those that make it happen. Earn the reputation as a doer, not a talker. Follow the principle of "under promising and over delivering". Look for creative and innovative ways to get the right things done,

and develop positive relationships with those who can help you get results.

6) **"Get Certified".** Earning professional certifications is one of the most valuable means to develop greater competence *and* earn credibility with others. Most professions have at least one professional certification you can earn.

Within the Mail profession, the Mail Systems Management Association (MSMA) has multiple certifications to consider pursuing: Mailpiece Design Consultant (MDC); Certified Mail & Distribution Systems Manager (CMDSM) and Certified Mail & Distribution Systems Supplier (CMDSS). Go to msmanational.org for details.

USPS also has a couple of worthwhile certifications: Executive Mail Center Management (EMCM) and Mailpiece Design Professional (MDP). Refer to usps.com for details.

7) **"Become a SME (Subject Matter Expert)".** Developing your personal expertise and willingly sharing it with others will earn you credibility. You can further develop your expertise by earning professional certifications, being active in trade associations, thoroughly reading trade publications, attending relevant conferences, and developing your own personal network of peers and industry leaders.

8) **"Develop a High Performance Team".** I have shared ways to build High Performance Teams in other lessons, such as lesson #12 *Is Your Team High-Performing or Hardly Performing?* One extensive research project boils down developing High Performance Teams into three keys: 1) Develop a sense of Fairness, 2) Develop a sense of Achievement and 3) Develop a sense of Camaraderie within the team.

9) **"Be a Fred"**. In lesson #22 I talk about the exceptional customer service provide by Fred the postal carrier. Going the extra mile and providing exceptional customer service will earn you and your team lasting credibility and success. Napoleon Hill was right when he said, "One of the most important principles of success is developing the habit of going the extra mile."

10) **"Promote Your Team's Accomplishments"**. We want to be known as servant leaders that focus the spotlight on our team's achievements. When leaders sincerely lift up our teams in the eyes of others, we ourselves are elevated in the minds of our teams and outsiders. We can promote our team's accomplishments through internal company communication channels (e.g. intra-net; company newsletter articles), open houses and tours, promotional team brochures, newsletters and through our local professional and trade associations.

Being a person of credibility is very rewarding for you and your team. Good luck to you on your journey!

39

Attitude is Contagious—
Is Yours Worth Catching?

"Your attitude, not your aptitude, will determine your altitude."
—Zig Ziglar, motivational speaker and writer

Our attitude as leaders is very important. Why? Our attitude may be the single biggest factor that determines our individual success (or lack thereof). Winston Churchill emphasized the importance of our attitude when he said, "Attitude is a little thing that makes a big difference."

The attitude we display at work will greatly influence the success levels of our teams. Our attitude speaks more than our words, as John Maxwell emphasized by saying, "People may hear your words, but they feel your attitude." Colin Powell adds, "I think whether you're having setbacks or not, the role of a leader is to always display a winning attitude."

Developing and maintaining a positive and optimistic attitude will greatly benefit us and our teams. How can we develop and keep our attitude positive and inspiring to others? Keep reading for some ideas that can help.

20 Keys to Having a Positive Attitude

Following is a list of 20 key principles that can help us develop and maintain positive attitudes. I suggest reviewing the list, and then selecting a few to intentionally take to heart and put into practice.

1) **Attitude Is a Choice.** Chuck Swindoll was right on target when he said, "The remarkable thing is, we have a choice every day regarding the attitude we will embrace for that day." Brian Tracy wisely says, "You cannot control what happens to you, but you can control your attitude toward what happens to you, and in that you will be mastering change rather than allowing it to master you."

2) **Be Positive, Proactive and Seize the Day.** There are two kinds of people in the world—positive people and negative people. Optimistic, positive people spring out of bed in the morning and say, "Good morning, Lord!" Pessimistic, negative people pull the covers over their heads and moan, "Good Lord, it's morning again!" What kind of person are you?   I agree with Thomas Jefferson, who said, "Nothing can stop the man (or woman) with the right mental attitude from achieving his (or her) goal; nothing on earth can help the man (or woman) with the wrong mental attitude."

3) **Keep an Attitude of Gratitude.** Being grateful for what we have will help keep us positive. I try to regularly say a prayer of thanks for the relationships, roles and responsibilities that I am privileged to have and for the life experiences that come my way. We all have lots to be thankful for, don't we? Marcus

Cicero emphasized that, "Gratitude is not only the greatest of virtues, but the parent of all others."

4) **Wait for Worry.** One study found that only 8 percent of the things we worry about come true. In the long run, problems look smaller. Nido Qubein encourages us to, "Cultivate the art of looking at events in their proper relationship to your whole life. Often something appears for the moment to be a tragedy, but it becomes only a minor annoyance when taken in the context of your total life."

5) **Have Goals and Visualize Success.** Identifying and working towards worthy goals—and taking time to celebrate progress along the way—will help keep our attitude positive. Having goals helps us be successful, as Earl Nightingale emphasized when he said, "People with goals succeed because they know where they're going."

It's important to visualize the successful realization of our goals. The quote from Henry Ford applies where he said, "Whether you say you can or say you can't, you are right either way."

6) **Embrace Changes.** Change is the one thing that we can count on, and in many cases change is needed to make things better. Try to see change as good and work to help changes achieve positive results.

7) **Play the Hand You Are Dealt**. You can't control who your parents were, or how much money your family had, or any physical shortcomings you were born with. But remember that the cards we were dealt are less important than how we play our hand. Booker T. Washington encouraged us, saying, "Success is to be measured not so much by the position that

one has reached in life as by the obstacles which he has overcome."

8) **Don't Be Afraid to Take Risks.** To be successful at life we must take some calculated risks and enjoy the successes and learn from the failures. Theodore Roosevelt said, "It is hard to fail, but it is worse never to have tried to succeed." And hockey great Wayne Gretzky reminded us that, "He missed every shot he did not take."

9) **Don't Let Mistakes and Failures Get You Down**. Do you make mistakes? Welcome to the human race. Making mistakes and experiencing temporary failures are perhaps the best teachers for us. The key is to analyze and reflect on our mistakes and failures and then apply the lessons learned.

10) **View Problems as Opportunities.** When problems arise we can let them get us down, or we can step up and look for ways to resolve them and make life better. Work-related problems normally need resolution, and by keeping positive and embracing the challenge to make things better we often can work problems through. It's also healthy to realize that we can't fix everything in the world around us. I like Saint Francis of Assisi's classic serenity prayer, "God grant me the serenity to accept the things I cannot change, the courage to the change the things I can, and the wisdom to know the difference."

11) **Try to Find Something Good in Everything.** Positive people look for the good in whatever life brings their way. Abraham Lincoln said, "We can complain because rose bushes have thorns, or rejoice because thorn bushes have roses."

12) **Remember That Health Is Your Wealth**. Josh Billings stated, "Health is like money, we never have a true idea of its value until we lose it." Living a healthy lifestyle will increase our energy, stamina and emotional well-being, and help us be more positive and effective in all that we do. A holistic, healthy lifestyle includes developing and using our mental capabilities (read a good book lately or taken a class just for the learning?). We are also spiritual beings, and finding faith and serving others can nourish our spiritual health.

13) **Surround Yourself with Positive Influences and Positive People.** We can read inspiring books and magazines. We can listen to positive and motivational recordings and speakers. We can attend positive and encouraging seminars and events. Years ago I was inspired by this quote from Charles Jones, "You are the same today that you are going to be in five years from now except for two things: the people with whom you associate and the books you read."

14) **Try to Improve Someone's Day.** Mother Teresa encouraged us to, "Let no one ever come to you without leaving better and happier." The more we reach out to help others, the better we feel about ourselves. I agree with Ralph Waldo Emerson when he said, "It is one of the beautiful compensations in life … that no man can sincerely try to help another without helping himself."

15) **Take Time to Do Things You Enjoy.** We all need times of rest, refreshment and recreation. All of us are different in the way we get refreshed and have our batteries re-charged. For me, I like to read, watch sports and get some exercise. I also

enjoy listening to music and hanging with family and friends. What do you enjoy?

16) **Laugh and Have Fun.** Laughter and having fun is good for us physically and emotionally and can help us keep positive. One of the reasons I like my daily newspaper is to read the comics and get a dose of humor.

17) **Learn to Say No.** It's good to live our lives in a way that benefits other people. At the same time we need to avoid burning ourselves out and therefore be of no good to anybody. One way to avoid burnout is to allow ourselves at times to say no to requests that may be too much for us at the given time.

18) **Be Comfortable in Your Own Skin.** It is less stressful to be ourselves, and not try to be someone we are not. People appreciate transparency and are repelled by phonies. It is important for is to be ourselves, but also to be our *best* self.

19) **Pursue a Purpose Bigger Than Yourself.** Robert Byrne said, "The purpose of life is a life of purpose." Living a life focused on significance is very rewarding and keeps us focused and grounded. For many of us, a life centered on the 3 Fs of Faith, Family and Friends keeps the bigger picture in mind and puts daily events in proper perspective.

   Part of a bigger purpose includes making a positive different in the world, as Martin Luther King encouraged when he said, "An individual has not started living until he can rise above the narrow confines of his individualistic concerns to the broader concerns of all humanity."

20) **Use the Most Powerful Force in the Universe.** There are a number of strong forces in the universe including things like hate, egotism and fear. But the strongest force in the universe

is love. True love goes far beyond mere emotion. Love is *a verb* that includes choice and expresses itself in behavior and actions. Jesus taught his followers to "Love your neighbor as yourself" and to "Love one another. As I have loved you, so you must love another." When we show love to others, we experience the ultimate win-win that Steven Covey advocated for. The recipient feels good and so do we.

Noted psychologist William James said, "The greatest discovery of my generation is that a human being can alter his life by altering his attitudes." Wade Boggs adds, "A positive attitude causes a chain reaction of positive thoughts, events and outcomes. It is a catalyst and it sparks extraordinary results." I wish you the best in developing and maintaining an attitude that is truly worth catching!

40

Why Ask Questions?

"The ability to ask the right question is more than half the battle of finding the answer."
—Thomas J. Watson, revolutionary CEO of IBM

Why should we ask questions? What are the keys to asking effective questions? What are some key questions we should be asking? Good questions indeed. Some of you are already expert at asking questions and reaping the benefits. Some of you are like me — we realize that we have room to improve in asking questions and using that tool to help us be better managers and make our teams more successful.

Let's dig in and explore some answers to the questions raised above.

Why Ask Questions?

Why should we ask questions? Here are some of the reasons why we should ask questions and why questions are so important:

1) **We only get answers to the questions we ask.** Asking questions is a great tool to find answers—and we never get answers to questions we never ask. Thomas Berger said, "The art and science of asking questions is the source of all knowledge."

2) **We ask questions to obtain information.** The primary purpose of asking a question is to obtain information. I resonate with Lou Holtz, who said, "I never learn anything talking. I only learn things when I ask questions."

3) **We ask questions to connect with people and show interest in them.** Perhaps the most effective way to connect with others is by asking questions. By asking questions we can find out more about people, which can help us build rapport, show empathy and build stronger relationships.

4) **We ask questions to cultivate humility.** It is wise for us to humble ourselves and seek knowledge and wisdom from others. Even King Solomon, perhaps the wisest man who ever lived, look at the enormity of his leadership responsibilities and said, "I am only a little child and do not know how to carry out my duties." Og Madino adds, "Take the attitude of a student, never too big to ask questions, never know too much to learn something new."

5) **We ask questions to ensure understanding or knowledge.** Questions can test for understanding and help clarify there is true understanding.

6) **We ask questions to encourage further thought.** Questions can be used to encourage people to think about something more deeply. Socrates was famous for asking questions to stimulate thinking and draw answers out of people that they never knew they had.

7) **Questions can help us build better ideas.** The old adage "two heads are better than one" applies when we are developing ideas. Asking questions can help us flesh out ideas and make them better than originally conveyed.

8) **Questions can challenge mind-sets and help us get out of ruts.** Questions can be the starting place to stimulate creative thinking, discovery and innovation.

What Are the Keys to Asking Effective Questions

Following are some keys to asking effective questions that will lead to the benefits described earlier:

- **Effective questions are open-ended, instead of yes/no questions.** The goal is to draw people and information out and get more complete responses.

- **When asking effective questions, it is important to listen and wait for the answer and not provide the answer.** Active listening motivates people to share more deeply and can help us better understand their answers.

- **Behind effective questioning is also the ability to listen to the answer and suspend judgment.** This means being intent on understanding what the person is really trying to say. This follows Stephen's Covey principle of "Seek first to understand, then to be understood".

- **Effective questioning includes thought-provoking questions that stimulate people to think and understand for themselves.** For example, when working with people to solve a problem, a good question might be, "What do you think the problem is?"

What Are Good Questions to Ask Ourselves as Leaders?

Here are some good questions to ask ourselves as leaders. I have adapted these questions from John Maxwell's book *Good Leaders Ask Great Questions*:

1) **Am I Investing in Myself? A Question of Personal Growth.** The most important investments we make are not financial, but the investments we make to develop ourselves so we can better serve others.

2) **Am I Genuinely Interested in Others? A Question of Motivation.** Motives matter. Are we primarily focused on helping ourselves—or helping others?

3) **Am I Grounded as a Leader? A Question of Stability.** One important component of being grounded is to be humble. Nobody likes following an arrogant leader. Rick Warren defined humility well when he said, "Humility is not denying your strengths. Humility is being honest about your weaknesses. All of us are a bundle of both great strengths and great weaknesses and humility is being able to be honest about both."

4) **Am I Adding Value to My Team? A Question of Teamwork.** John Wooden was quoted as saying there was one question he asked himself every day: "How can I make my team better?"

5) **Am I Staying in My Strength Zone? A Question of Effectiveness.** Sometimes we have responsibilities that force us out of our strength areas. But research shows we are far more effective when we spend the majority of our time operating in our strength zones. Samuel Johnson was right when he said, "Almost every man wastes part of his life in attempts to display qualities he does not possess."

6) **Am I Taking Care of Today? A Question of Success.** Every day consists of 1,440 minutes that we can waste away ... or make them count. I am encouraged by the words of John Wooden when he shared the advice from his father to, "Make every day your masterpiece." Making time every day in Stephen Covey's *Quadrant Two* is important—doing things that are "important but not urgent" such as planning, building relationships, developing our faith, learning, and taking care of our health.

What Are Good Questions to Ask Our Team Members?

Robert Half said, "Asking the right questions takes as much skill as giving the right answers." I want to leave you with some potentially good questions to ask your team members at relevant times:

1) **What do you think?**
2) **How can I serve you?**
3) **Did we meet or exceed expectations?**
4) **What can we do to make the team even more successful?**
5) **What did you learn from this experience?**
6) **Did we add value to our stakeholders?**
7) **How could I help make your job better?**
8) **What do I need to know?**
9) **What am I missing?**
10) **If you were the boss, what is the one change you would make?**

Here is a final quote from Anthony Robbins: "Successful people ask better questions, and as a result, they get better results." I wish you and your team the best of success as you ask better questions and get better results!

41

Mentoring: Our Passport to Building a Lasting Legacy

"We all leave a legacy. The only question is what kind of legacy will we leave—positive or negative?"
—Wes Friesen

Perhaps the greatest legacy any of us can leave is the people whose potential we helped develop. A great tool for developing people—and yourself—is mentoring. There are many benefits to being in a mentoring relationship. A mentoree gains valuable insight, a listening ear and sounding board, understanding of strengths, opportunities for improvement, different perspective, doors opened, and more.

The mentor often gains more than the mentoree, including such gifts as the opportunity to pass on life lessons learned, practice interpersonal and management skills, expand their horizons, and the satisfaction of helping another person achieve their potential. An effective mentor looks at how he or she can benefit others, and this ultimately benefits the individuals and the larger organization.

Suggested steps when starting a mentoring relationship include:

1) **Clarify and Communicate Clear Expectations.** Make sure both the mentor and mentoree are on the same page and supportive of each other's expectations.

2) **Set Realistic Goals & Objectives.** Collaboratively setting goals in the front-end will help ensure focus and also builds direction and accountability into the relationship.

3) **Focus on cultivating a great relationship.** I like the following Ben Stein quote: "Personal relationships are the fertile soil from which all advancement, all success, all achievement in real life grows." Ultimately the main lasting benefit from mentoring is the development of a positive, win-win relationship between the two parties.

4) **Seek opportunities to maintain contact.** It takes time together to nourish healthy relationships. Schedule regular one-on-one meetings, but also look for other opportunities to spend time together and learn from each other.

5) **Develop a mentoring network.** There is real value to having multiple informal and formal mentors that can help us grow and develop. On the other side, being involved in helping multiple people develop is very rewarding and helps build that positive legacy that lives beyond our time in the organization.

The Seven E's of Effective Mentoring

At a National Postal Forum conference I heard my friend Jim Burns do an excellent presentation on mentoring. Part of what Jim included was the "7 E's" of effective mentoring, which came from Tony Dungy. Tony is the highly respected and successful retired coach of the champion Indianapolis Colts. Following are Tony's seven keys to being an effective mentor:

1) **Engage.** It's impossible to mentor from a distance. Without engagement, you cannot lead effectively. One way to facilitate engagement is to have an open-door policy with your mentoree. Let her know you want to be there as needed and encourage a connection if a special need arises. Another tool is to practice MBWA ("management by walking around"). Spending some time in the world of your mentoree helps promote engagement and shows that you care.

2) **Educate.** Education is an essential building block of effective mentorship. Mentoring should about helping others become the best they can be, and that is built on a foundation of helping, guiding and teaching. Our goal is to help everyone we are mentoring to earn an "A"—whatever an "A" represents in your organization.

3) **Equip.** Effective mentors help create an environment in which others can be productive and excel. Equipping goes hand in hand with education in helping people perform to their highest potential.

4) **Encourage.** Encouragement is the fuel that powers our efforts to engage, educate and equip. Encouragement helps lubricate the rough spots that people go through. As J.R.R Tolkien said, "Kind and encouraging words cost little but are worth much."

5) **Empower.** True empowerment is preparation followed by the appropriate freedom. The best way to learn is by doing, so there comes a point when we need to let people loose to do their jobs.

6) **Energize.** The best leaders and mentors energize and inspire those they are leading. Tools include having an inspiring and compelling vision, clearing road blocks to success,

and believing in people and treating them like adults—
not children.

7) **Elevate.** Raising up other people is the truly selfless goal of
every effective mentor. It's not about getting the credit; it's
about helping the organization and every person in it be the
best they can be. As President Harry S. Truman put it, "It
is amazing how much you can accomplish when it doesn't
matter who gets the credit."

Mentoring can truly be a win-win if you work at doing it well. I
agree with Steve Washington (COO and Co-founder of Casentric)
when he stressed, "Mentoring is a two-way street. You get out what
you put in." I also appreciate Benjamin Disraeli's thought, "The
greatest good you can do for another is not just share your riches,
but to reveal to him his own."

Wes's Personal Mentor Story

I have the privilege and benefits of being in multiple mentoring
relationships, both as a "mentor" and as a "mentoree". I want to share
one very personal story which illustrates the power of mentoring.

August 23, 2003 was by far the worst day of my long business
career. On that day I had one of my Supervisors (Mike) not report to
work that morning. I had only known and worked with Mike for one
year, but I knew he was very reliable and something was amiss. To
make a long story short, I eventually got hold of his wife and learned
the tragic news that Mike had taken his life that day.

As you can imagine I was devastated when I heard the news.
Even with all my experience and education, I was at a loss of what to
do. So I called my mentor, Joe McArthur. Joe was a very experienced

Vice President of my company, and we had started a mentoring relationship as part of a Management Development program.

Joe told me to head down to his office, and he would guide me through this. He had been through three prior suicides in his career, and could share what he learned on dealing with this extremely challenging situation. I am eternally indebted to Joe, and this story shows the power of having someone more experienced and wiser than you to serve as a mentor and show you the ropes.

Let me close with a classic Winston Churchill quote: "We make a living by what we get; we make a life by what we give." Good luck as you give of yourself to help develop other people in your life. They will be blessed—as so will you!

42

Conferences: Your Secret Weapon for Management Success

"Learning is not attained by chance, it must be sought for with ardor and attended to with diligence."
— Abigail Adams

As I originally wrote this, I was preparing to speak and attend the Fall MAILCOM conference (mailcom-conference.com). Previously that year I had spoken at and attended the National Postal Forum, and a couple of other conferences. Many have found that the "secret weapon" to being a successful manager in any industry or profession is to attend conferences and draw deeply from the potential value they bring.

When I receive the opportunity to manage a new area that I'm not familiar with, I look for internal and external resources to learn and gain competence. In terms of external resources, I look for trade associations, trade journals, professional certifications, and at least one relevant conference.

One of the newest areas I now manage is credit and collections. I was fortunate to discover the National Association of Credit Management (NACM; web-site www.NACM.org). I quickly joined NACM, and strongly endorse NACM for every credit professional. NACM has local chapters, sponsors webinars and on-line classes, publishes a quality trade journal, has top-notch certification programs—and sponsors a valuable annual conference called *Credit Congress*.

Getting the approval to attend important conferences has always been challenging—even more so under when economic conditions are not ideal. But actively participating in conferences is a key to success for you as a professional in your industry, and is important to the success of your organization. So how can you obtain approval to attend conferences? Here are some ideas:

Keys to Get Approval to Attend Conferences

Approval often comes down to the ROI to your organization—are the benefits worth the costs? Before discussing benefits, let's start with the costs. There are ways to lower the cost to attend. First, for those in the Mail Industry, if you are a Mail Systems Management Association (MSMA) member you qualify for a MSMA discount for the MAILCOM conference. Both MAILCOM and National Postal Forum offer a discount for early registration as do many other conferences.

Second, you can shop around for the least expensive transportation method. Attendees will often double up on rooms to cut that cost. I know of a number of attendees that will offer to pay some or all of the travel costs out of their pockets. People who do that look at it as an investment in their careers, and it shows your management chain how committed you are to developing yourself and adding value to your organization.

The biggest key to getting approval is to explain the return (benefits) to you and your organization. Here are some benefits that you can tailor to your own situation:

1) **Learning Ways to Reduce Costs and Improve Efficiency**. You will learn updated information on how to minimize costs (such as postage and shipping costs), and learn ideas to improve the efficiency of your operations. I have seen my organization and others save thousands and even millions of dollars via learning and implementing work share postal discounts, shape based pricing, targeted mailing, cleaner addressing and reduction of undeliverable mail, intelligent/selective inserting, full-service intelligent mail discounts, applying QR 2D bar codes, implementing six sigma and lean principles—the list goes on and on.

2) **Learning Best Practices and Ideas for Process Improvements.** You will learn from the industry's top experts, peers and vendors in the exhibit hall the Best Practices of the country's leading high performance organizations. You will also hear ideas about process improvements that can drive improved efficiency, effectiveness and quality. You will learn how to improve quality, have more sustainable operations, and eliminate waste. Included can be practical tips related to billing, work flow, job design, process analysis and ergonomics.

3) **Learn about the Latest Technology, Automation and other Tools**. Conferences are great sources to hear about the latest relevant technology from the speakers, peers and vendors.

Often you will get ideas for significant cost savings and improved operations from wise investments in equipment and software. Here is the chance to see what might be of value to your organization. You can visit the exhibit hall and expand your list of vendor and supplier contacts for current and future reference.

4) **Build a Strong Network and Support Group.** Conferences provide an opportunity to meet the industry's top leaders and experts first hand. One of the great features of this conference is how approachable the speakers are. Also, there are many opportunities to network with peers from around the country — then build your own professional support group.

5) **Become Inspired to Succeed.** The keynote and seminar speakers will inspire you to push even harder to help your organization be more successful. The top conferences are noted for their wide selection of seminars, including those aimed at our personal and leadership development.

6) **Add More Value to Your Key Stakeholders.** The investors of your organization will benefit from the cost savings and efficiencies that you adopt. In addition, you can learn ways to add more value to your customers and improve customer satisfaction and favorability.

The best conferences also offer a number of sessions geared to leadership and management best practices, and proven ways to provide more positive work environments for your employees that will drive improved morale, motivation and performance.

7) **Improve your Credibility within the Industry and your Organization.** You will learn important information that will

benefit you personally—and your organization. As you go home and apply what you know you will gain greater respect and recognition.

In addition, at many conferences you can earn professional certificates. For example, while at MAILCOM you can take advantage of the opportunity to earn the professional certifications sponsored by MSMA, including the MDC: Mailpiece Design Consultant; CMDSM: Certified Mail Distribution System Manager or CMDSS: Certified Mail Distribution Systems Suppliers. Note: for more information about these programs visit msmanational.org.

8) **Become a Teacher, Inspire Others and Build a Stronger Team.** With all the learning, networking and inspiration you receive, you will be equipped to go back home and inspire and teach others. This will be rewarding to you – and your team!

One final tip: if you do attend a conference, make sure you prepare a written report and share with your boss and team. Also do a verbal presentation of the key highlights from your report, and let your excitement show through about what you gained at the conference.

Good luck as you pursue getting approval to join me or other professionals at future conferences!

Conclusion

Anthony J. D'Angelo counseled us to, "Develop a passion for learning. If you do, you will never cease to grow." My great-aunt Tina modeled a life-long passion for learning that has inspired me.

Tina was a Pastor's widow, and quite frankly knew the Bible better than the vast majority of Pastors. She led Bible studies, taught Sunday School classes, and freely shared her vast knowledge.

But Tina was not content to rest on her laurels when it came to her knowledge. She was constantly taking correspondence classes from schools like Moody School of the Bible, in an attempt to keep learning! And I recall her sharing with me her excitement when she would get an "A" on a term paper or an exam. (I found it somewhat amusing, because in my mind she likely knew as much if not more than the professor!)

She stopped taking classes at age 91, and only stopped because of her deteriorating eyesight and health. There was a popular commercial that encouraged us to be "like Mike". I want to be "like Tina"!

I truly hope you have enjoyed the lessons in this book, and will share relevant lessons with your teammates and other leaders you know. Hopefully you have found many nuggets of key concepts that can help you and your team continue to improve.

Here is one final quote for you from Leonardo da Vinci: "I have been impressed with the urgency of doing. Knowing is not enough; we must apply. Being willing is not enough; we must do." My best to you as you apply what you know, and then watch yourself and your team soar to new heights of performance!

Appendix A

The Ultimate Servant Leader

Robert K. Greenleaf coined the term *servant leadership* in the 1970s and is the author of several articles and books on the topic. He founded the Greenleaf Center for Servant Leadership. Greenleaf stated:

> Servant leadership begins with the natural feeling that one wants to serve, to serve first. Then conscious choice brings one to aspire to lead...The difference manifests itself in the care taken by the servant – first to make sure other people's highest priority needs are being served. The best test ...is: do those served grow as persons; do they while being served, become healthier, wiser, freer, more autonomous, more likely themselves to become servants?

Greenleaf may have popularized the term and concepts in the 1970s, but the original servant leader and the ultimate practitioner lived 2,000 years ago. Jesus Christ is arguably the most influential person and leader that has ever walked on the earth—in part evidenced that 2,000 years after he was on earth, more than 2 billion people claim to be His followers.

Jesus taught and modeled what servant leadership is intended to be. Following are some of the key teachings as recorded in the Bible:

> "The greatest among you will be your servant. For whoever exalts himself will be humbled, and who-ever humbles himself will be exalted" (Matthew 23:11–12 NIV).

> Jesus called them (His apostles) together and said, "You know that those who are regarded as rulers of the Gentiles lord it over them, and their high officials exercise authority over them. Not so with you. Instead, whoever wants to be become great among you must be your servant, and whoever wants to be first must be slave of all. For even the Son of Man (Jesus) did not come to be served, but to serve, and to give His life as a ransom for many."

Jesus modeled being a servant leader on many occasions, including the famous incident of humbling Himself to wash His disciple's feet:

> … When Jesus had finished washing the disciples' feet, he put on his outer clothes and returned to his place. "Do you understand what I have done for you?" he asked them. You call me 'Teacher' and 'Lord', and rightly so for that is what I am. Now that I, your Lord and Teacher, have washed your feet, you also should

wash one another's feet. I have set you an example
that you should do as I have done for you. I tell you
the truth, no servant is greater than his master, nor is
a messenger greater than the one who sent him. Now
that you know these things you will be blessed if you
do them." (John 13:1–17 NIV)

If servant leadership worked well for Jesus, seems like it will
work for us too!

Personal Note

Not only is Jesus the great Servant Leader. For people like me He
is my personal Savior. He offers the gift of salvation and a personal
eternal relationship to anyone who desires this. In Jesus' words:

"For God so loved the world that he gave his one and
only Son, that whoever believes in Him shall not
perish but have eternal life. For God did not send his
Son into the world to condemn the world, but to save
the world through Him." (John 3:16–17 NIV)

The Apostle Paul explained, "All have sinned and fall short of the
glory of God ... For the wages of sin is death, but the gift of God is
eternal life in Christ Jesus our Lord." (Romans 3:23; 6:23 NIV). The
Apostle John summed up how to start a personal relationship with
Jesus when he said, "Yet to all who received him (Jesus), to those that
believed in his name, he gave the right to become children of God"
(John 1:12 NIV). I believed in and received Jesus as my Savior as a
seven year-old boy and it was the best decision I ever made!

Appendix B

Wes's Recommended Leadership & Management Books

Following is a list of some books with valuable insights on leadership, management and building high performance teams. There are obviously other good books on these topics, but these are some of my favorites over the years.

Lead With Humility: 12 Leadership Lessons from Pope Francis (Jeffrey A. Adams)

Great Leadership (Anthony Bell)

On Becoming a Leader (Warren Bennis)

Leading at a Higher Level and *The Secret: What Great Leaders Know & Do* (Ken Blanchard)

Execution (Larry Bossily & Ram Charan)

First, Break All the Rules (Marcus Buckingham & Curt Coffman)

Now Discover Your Strengths (Marcus Buckingham & Donald O. Clifton)

The One Thing You Need to Know … About Great Managing, Great Leading and

Sustained Individual Success (Marcus Buckingham)

Good to Great (Jim Collins)

The Speed of Trust (Stephen M.R. Covey)

The 7 Habits of Highly Effective People (Stephen R. Covey)

Creating Magic (Lee Cockerell)

Leadership is an Art (Max DePree)

The Effective Executive (Peter Drucker)

Leadership (Rudolph W. Giuliani)

The Carrot Principle (Adrian Gostick & Chester Elton)

The Servant and *The Most Powerful Leadership Principle: How to Become a Servant Leader* (James C. Hunter)

The Leadership Challenge (James M. Kouzes & Barry Z. Posner)

Patrick Lenconi's leadership fables: "The Five Temptations of a CEO", "The Five

Dysfunctions of a Team", "Death by Meeting", "The Four Obsessions of an Extraordinary Executive", "Silo, Politics and Turf Wars", "The Three Signs of a Miserable Job"

Love Works (Joel Manby)

The Disciplined Leader (John Manning)

How to Impact and Influence Others: 9 Keys to Successful Leadership (James Merritt)

Getting Results (Clinton O. Longenbecker & Jack L. Simonetti)

The 21 Irrefutable Laws of Leadership, *The Leadership Handbook*, and *The 360 Degree Leader* (John Maxwell)

Leadership: Theory and Practice (Peter G. Northouse)

How Full is Your Bucket (Tom Rath & Donald O. Clifton)

The Contrarian's Guide to Leadership (Steven B. Sample)

The Enthusiastic Employee (Sirota, Mischkind & Meltzer)

Leadership Brand (Dave Ulrich & Norm Smallwood)

The 12 Elements of Great Managing (Rodd Wagner & James K. Harter)

Leading with Integrity (Pat Williams)

Notes

Lesson 9

1. From *Leading with Integrity*, page 107, published by Barbour Publishing, Inc. Used by permission. This is an excellent book by Pat Williams, which I highly recommend for exploring more deeply the leadership wisdom of Solomon.

2. Ibid., 166.

Lesson 12

1. Results of a Gallup Survey reported January 28, 2015 (Gallup.com)

2. By Sirota consulting group, documented in the book *The Enthusiastic Employee* by Sirota, Mischind and Meltzer.

Lesson 16

1. The Ten Rules have been adapted from John J. Murphy's book *Pulling Together*

Lesson 17

1. Statistics from 2015 Hay Group's global normative data base and client business metrics (haygroup.com)

Lesson 18

1. Statistics reported by Gallup in January 28, 2015 from their employee engagement survey (Gallup.com)

Lesson 20

1. Statistics reported by Gallup in January 28, 2015 from their employee engagement survey (Gallup.com)

Lesson 21

1. Statistics reported by Gallup in January 28, 2015 from their employee engagement survey (Gallup.com)

Lesson 23

1. Story was cited by Dale Carnegie in his book *How to Win Friends and Influence People*

Lesson 36

1. Society of Human Resource Managers 2012 survey
2. Chicago Tribune 2013 survey
3. US Department of Labor research referenced by Chapman and White

About the Author

Wes Friesen is the Manager of Billing, Credit & Payments for a large utility in the Northwest. He currently serves or has served on a number of professional or non-profit Boards or national Committees for organizations such as: Junior Achievement, Utility Executive Course, Mail Systems Management Association, The Association for Work Process Improvements, Love India Mission Endeavor, National Postal Customer Council, Greater Portland Postal Customer Council, GracePointe Church, and others.

Wes and his teams have earned a wide variety of awards and certifications from, and been featured by a variety of organizations including MAILCOM, Mail Magazine, In-Plant Print & Mail Association, Mail Systems Management Association, National Association of Printing Leadership, United States Postal Service, In-Plant Graphics, and Greater Portland Postal Customer Council. Wes received the prestigious Franklin Award in 2010 from MAILCOM for his contributions to the mail communications industry.

Wes is an award-winning University Instructor and taught for several universities, most recently at George Fox University. He is a featured and award-winning speaker at a variety of regional and national conferences. Wes has had articles published by Business Credit, Finance Matters, In-Plant Graphics, Mail Magazine, Today Journal, Mailing Systems & Technology, Document, Perspectives and Inside Edge. He writes a "Real Life Management" column for "Mailing Systems and Technology".

Wes earned a B.S. in Business Administration from George Fox University, and an MBA from the University of Portland. He has also earned 14 different business professional certifications including: CCE, CBF, CBA, CFM, CMA, CTP, CMDSM, EMCM, MCOM, MDC, CM, PHR, APP, and ICP.

Wes lives in Portland, Oregon with his wife Debi, and has two daughters, a son-in-law and a granddaughter. He enjoys reading, walking, tennis, traveling, and follows several sports teams.

Wes has a personal website where you can download free information: wesfriesen.com

HOW TO CONTACT WES:

If you would like to schedule Wes for a speaking engagement, please contact him!

Wes Friesen
P.O. Box 2575
Clackamas, OR 97015
E-mail: wesmfriesen@gmail.com
Cell #: 971-806-0812
Work #: 503-612-4771

TO PURCHASE ADDITIONAL COPIES OF
YOUR TEAM CAN SOAR!
You can purchase additional copies of the book from:
- XulonPress.com/bookstore
- An online retailer
- From Wes directly (if you want to make a bulk purchase, it's recommended to contact Wes about quantity discounts)

CPSIA information can be obtained
at www.ICGtesting.com
Printed in the USA
FSOW04n1701270116
16257FS